1

Praying the Pattern
the Lord's Prayer as framework for prayer and life

by
Andii Bowsher

Praying the Pattern
the Lord's Prayer as framework for prayer and life

Copyright © Andii Bowsher 2005,

First published in Great Britain 2005 by Andii Bowsher

AbbeyNous Press

Biblical quotations are from the NRSV.
ISBN 1-905452-10-1

The website associated with this book is
http://abbeynous.schtuff.com/
Further copies can be obtained from
http://www.pabd.co.uk/

Table of Contents

Introduction.

There are lots of books on the Lord's Prayer. Most of them are reflections on the meanings of the phrases and the significance of the prayer. Many of them are scholarly and dealing with questions of origins, language, semantics, textual histories and histories of usage. This book is not one of those. I have read my share of such books and they have informed my thinking in various ways. However, the real focus of what is written here is how to pray the prayer. I may have missed it but it does seem that there is not a great deal available that takes the Lord's Prayer as a pattern and framework for prayer and tries to explore a little how to make that work in our praying together and singly and perhaps to push out a little into developing the prayer as a pattern for spirituality.

To understand why I might want to invite you to do this, let me tell you a little bit about how this concern was formed. When I was in the Christian nurture stage of my faith and wondering how I should pray, a number of suggestions, books and pamphlets came my way to help me to pray. I seem to recall that many of them said that we should talk to God 'naturally'. I gathered that this meant that it was not necessary to learn a new dialect or set of vocabulary to talk to God, what we already knew was alright and perhaps preferable because it was in some way being ourselves before God. There were a number of people and books that suggested also that when we talked to God we might find it helpful to have an agenda or a pattern to go through different kinds of things like confession, adoration, thanksgiving and supplication. Or there might be acronymic variants like "ACTS" -adoration, confession, thanksgiving, supplication. Clearly it was felt that having a framework was helpful for at least some personalities.

On reflection, it seemed that several models of praying were competing for attention here: one which was about friendly conversation which was being implicitly contrasted with a model of formal ritual words being exchanged and then there was a model which was either about a meeting with an agenda or perhaps the idea of a balanced diet and regular nutrition where the right amount of all the food groups was needed to ensure a healthy growth. Over the years I found quite a lot of tension or even argument between people about which way we should pray, which was more authentically Christian and which was sub-Christian or unsound. Interestingly enough the preferences seemed to go in the direction our culture was taking; towards favouring the spontaneous and informal.

Now I would definitely not see them as in competition; more a matter of what is appropriate. It is clear that we use various patterns of conversation between human beings and so it is no bad thing to see them used between ourselves and God. Sometimes it may be good to approach God intimately as a good friend, at other times we do need an agenda. Sometimes a matter of fact approach is good, at others a love song may be appropriate or a poem -just like with other people. Sometimes we are spontaneous, sometimes we need to be deliberate and planned. I guess that most of the ideas in this book are of necessity about the more planned, structured and less spontaneous praying that we might do. Naturally, a framework for prayer is going to be towards that end of the scale.

Many years later I find myself wondering why it was that so many outline frameworks for prayer have been commended but the most Dominical and scriptural one of all for Christians wasn't. In short; how is it that we have so often missed using the Lord's prayer in this way; as a pattern prayer? It is beyond the scope of this book to investigate the historical answer to that question, suffice to say that it looks, at first sight, as if quite early on the Lord's Prayer came to be treated as a set prayer to be used in a similar way to the recitation of the Shema by faithful Jews, rather than a pattern.

There does seem to be some reason to take this a plausible origin for the practice of treating the Lord's Prayer as a set-piece prayer. Jewish practice was to say the Shema ("Hear O Israel the LORD our God is the only Lord and you shall love ....") three times a day, morning, noon and afternoon, and there is evidence to suggest that Christians took to saying the Lord's prayer three times a day morning, noon and afternoon, probably in imitation or continuation of Jewish practice. In such circumstances it seems likely that needing an equivalent to the Shema, the Lord's prayer was felt to be a suitable substitute recitation.

In this book the aim is to provoke action and to that end to offer some ways to use the Lord's prayer as a prayer pattern. I want to make a strong appeal for the Lord's prayer to gain a fuller and more central place in our devotional lives if only because I think that we should take seriously that it is the Lord's prayer and that as such it should command a greater degree of time and usage in our praying singly and corporately than it probably does. To all intents and purposes the Lord's Prayer is peripheral to our praying and usually only gets employed when it is considered an appropriate moment, like ending or beginning a prayer meeting, or because it is in a particular liturgy at a certain point. I have rarely, if ever, attended a prayer event (other than those I have organised with this agenda in mind) where the Lord's Prayer is at all a shaping influence on the proceedings or even exercises any discernible influence on the prayers of individuals themselves. It seems that the Lord's Prayer does not significantly shape the praying consciousness of Christians. I speak from many years attendance at prayer meetings, services and other events in which corporate Christian praying is encouraged as part of the proceedings. The lack of use of the Lord's Prayer in ordinary practice as a pattern or framework prayer, seems to me strange given that we are meant to be following Christ's teaching and that this is a twice-repeated piece of practical-example teaching from Jesus himself.

The effect of simply seeing it as a 'set-piece' prayer seems to be to marginalise it by placing it in a mental category along with other set-piece prayers like that of St.Francis ("Make me a channel of your peace...") or of St.Richard of Chichester ("... to see you more clearly , love you more dearly, follow you more nearly day be day..."). It is then only really used for moments when a set-piece prayer is called for or when it is felt appropriate to give some kind of sense of connection to Jesus's teaching on prayer, such as in the Communion services of a number of churches where it is introduced between the Eucharistic prayer and the receiving of communion with words like,

"As our Saviour taught us, so we pray" or similar. It appears that the net effect of this is to make the Lord's Prayer an occasional feature of our praying rather than a vital in-former of our praying. The intention behind this book is to encourage us to make sure that the Lord's Prayer to shapes and directs our praying on a regular basis.

In what follows are offered some ways that could help us to use the Lord's prayer more fully, frequently and in a variety of situations. I offer these ideas and exercises in the hope that individuals and groups can grow in relation to God through them. In writing I have been thinking of those who lead and participate in small groups where prayer is most of or part of the agenda for the group and also of people who day by day pray without the physical presence of others and find a structure helpful. It is a call to experiment and there is an accompanying website where ideas and 'results' can be shared and further ideas developed or offered. The site is at http://abbeynous.schtuff.com/ .

A note on language

As you read you may from time to time notice that a 'He' or 'Him' you might be expecting in referring to God does not appear and the word 'God' will appear again. This is because I have tried to avoid specifying God as having a gender as far as possible and I have felt that God can be God's own pronoun. After all God is beyond genders; both male and female image God and in any case God is both personal and more than personal. I have for a number of years worked among people for whom gender issues are understandably very important. I have tried to write in a way that would gain their trust and not alienate unnecessarily. I do realise, however, that it is possible that some other readers might find this irritating. All I can do is ask your indulgence of those of us who find gender-specific and uninclusive language disturbing, off-putting and difficult to commend to our peers whom we would like to be able to encourage into a positive relationship with Christ..

Getting our Bearings.

Before introducing the ideas and exercises, it may be helpful to show the approach that has been taken to understanding the Lord's Prayer.

The approach has been the main one guiding the formulation of ideas and using the prayer devotionally. It may be that various readers take a different line in understanding the biblical texts of the Lord's Prayer. The aim here is not so much as to argue for this particular set of interpretations of the prayer, but to help us to take the 'Paternoster' into our own praying. It is my hope, therefore, that if you do think that it should be understood differently, you will still be able to pick up some of the ideas about how to pray and rework them to fit into your own framework of understanding the prayer. I would be very interested to hear what those adaptations are and would encourage you to share them with me and others through the 'Abbey Nous' website.

Starting in the Gospels.

There are two passages where the Lord's prayer appears; one in Matthew (6.9-13) in the sermon on the mount; the other in Luke (11.2-4) in a different context of less fully public teaching. The wording is not quite the same and the presented occasion of the teaching is likewise not the same.

In the Matthew version (which is the basis for what we normally use liturgically as a set prayer), the context is Jesus's teaching on prayer following warnings about the spiritual peril of praying for show and making wordy or long-winded prayers. It is generally accepted that is constitutes a strong steer towards seeing the Lord's prayer as a pattern rather than something to be 'babbled'. The use of the Lord's Prayer as a liturgical set-piece seems to go against the general tenor of the passages around it in the Sermon on the Mount. The strange thing is that despite this general agreement that this is the right kind of way to understand the Lord's Prayer in the passage, it never seems to get out of the commentaries and into liturgical or use in informal prayer meetings. The principles of not babbling or showing-off in prayer are taught (but not often enforced, it must be said) but the idea of using the framework of the Lord's prayer is not.

In Luke it is much more arguable that it could be taken to be a set prayer. Jesus teaches the prayer in response to a disciple's request to be taught to pray. The request appears to have been prompted by observing Jesus at prayer and by an awareness that John taught his followers to pray. Offsetting the set-prayer interpretation of this passage, it is thought likely that John, following the tradition of other Jewish teachers, had taught his disciples a prayer that they would pray together and that Jesus's disciples wanted to have a group prayer too. Most such prayers in Jesus' time are thought to have been framework prayers rather than set prayers. Clearly Luke's version is shorter and contains fewer clauses than Matthew's, perhaps more suited to using it in a group context as a framework.

There is a lot of similarity between the two instances of the prayer. They follow the same order and deal broadly with the same topics. It seems reasonable to use them each to illuminate the meaning of the other and to presume that the same basic principles underlie them. Let's look at the two versions together.

[Mat 6:9]"Pray then in this way:	[Luke 11:2] He said to them, "When you pray, say:
Our Father in heaven, hallowed be your name.	Father, hallowed be your name.
[10]Your kingdom come. Your will be done, on earth as it is in heaven.	Your kingdom come.
[11]Give us this day our daily bread.	[3]Give us each day our daily bread.
[12]And forgive us our debts, as we also have forgiven our debtors	[4]And forgive us our sins, for we ourselves forgive everyone indebted to us.
[13] And do not bring us to the time of trial, but rescue us from the evil one."	And do not bring us to the time of trial."

This shows clearly that they are from a common source yet expressed differently, they have a common structure but some variation. All of which suggests strongly that the exact form of words is not important so much as the basic outline and the theme of each clause.

It may be that Matthew's version reflects a more Hebrew sense of 'sacred poetry' where saying the same thing in a different way occurs. We see this kind of 'rhyming' of the meaning or the sense of a line rather than of the sound of words in the line in many of the Psalms. For example towards the end of Psalm 139, the words "Search me O God and know my heart" is paralleled by the following line "Test me an know my anxious thoughts". Note how they cover roughly the same semantic ground but develop the meaning slightly differently to reinforce and explain the other line. It is as if it is a kind of semantic rhyme rather than a phonetic rhyme.

Looked at in this way, what Luke writes down as "Your Kingdom come" is given more elaboration in Matthew, where the addition of "Your will be done on earth as it is in heaven" enables us to understand better how to pray "your kingdom come". Likewise, not being brought to the time of trial is explained further by Matthew's extension: "but rescue us from the evil one". These are not extra ideas so much as explanations or supporting phrases of the one preceding. For this reason, in this book, the 'Matthew additions' are included in the general sense of each clause rather than as additional 'headings' for prayer.

Clauses.
Let's now go through the prayer phrase by phrase looking at the things which can't help us to make use of the prayer for ourselves.

'[Our] Father'. Almost certainly underlying this phrase is Jesus's fairly distinctive personal use of the Aramaic "Abba" to address God. It has proven difficult to translate it into English since our usual main alternatives are either likely to fall on the side of being too reverential or formal in feel -"father" -which few of us would normally use to address our fathers- or too childish in the wrong kind of sense: "Daddy" normally doesn't feel quite grown up enough for most users of British English. We seem to be encouraged, then, to aim for a sense of intimacy along with a sense of reverence.

Luke simply has "Father/Daddy" unadorned and solitary. Matthew has "Our" added which points us to the solidarity both with Christ and with one another. We do not pray this prayer alone: it is prayed with Christ first of all; our praying is at the heart of Godhead in Christ. And in Christ all our brothers and sisters are with us.

Here, then, we are invited to approach God with intimacy and reverence recognising our solidarity with others and Christ's solidarity with us. 'Approach' is probably more important than we normally give credit for. I once had a badge that said "Sudden prayers make God jump". Mainly I had it because it was absurd and so it amused me. In reality, I felt sure, God can't be taken by surprise like that. I am sure that God's relationship with time is not the same as our relationship with time and that the idea of taking God by surprise is in actual fact pretty meaningless. I suspect a more accurate picturing of God's relationship to our praying is not of failing to attend to us and therefore being surprised when we do pray; rather God is attending to us all of the time (that is to say 'all of our time') and eagerly attentive to our direct address. Sudden prayers reveal our having not been in conscious communion with God. What to us are sudden prayers, are simply another aspect of who we are before God.

However, ploughing in without some kind of preparation is sometimes, perhaps often, not good for us as praying beings. Being embodied people who understand the world through our senses and by our location in spacetime, we tend to have strategies of relating to God by analogy and metaphor drawing on our habitual experience of the world. So imagining ourselves to be coming before God or to be acknowledging the presence of God like a friend whom we have just become aware is sitting with us or likening prayer to picking up a telephone, are ways that can help us to make a transition from not explicitly and consciously addressing God to giving our focussed attention to God. So, 'Our Father' can help us to begin to focus on God, to mark to ourselves that we are engaged in an activity that is different in some way to to what we were doing before and will be doing after.

That is not necessarily to say that we were and will be ignoring God. It may well be that activities undertaken for God and within the will of God are undertaken without conscious focus on God at every moment. In some cases trying to focus exclusively on God as we do something could be dangerous (if we are driving round a particularly difficult road system, for example) or at least jeopardise what it is we are attempting to do (if we are trying to mark a student's essay fairly and clearly). It is right and proper that some activities be undertaken in the knowledge that we work and act before the face of God and the faithful carrying out of our calling is itself an offering to God, an act of worship. Focusing on God is not always appropriate. God is in any case everywhere and undergirds all that is. Proper attention to things in a life that is oriented to worship and service of God is to find God in all things.

The choice of words as we begin our conscious, focused attention to God can show what kind of analogy or metaphor for the encounter with God we might, perhaps, unconsciously, be using. Alternatively it can be a way to set the scene for ourselves mentally. It is likely, then, that 'Father' will have some different feelings and moods associated with it to 'Our Father' and even to 'heavenly Father, and that is before we consider adding other adjectives like 'almighty' or 'ever-loving' or even thinking about the gender issues that it raises for at least some people.

'Hallowed be ...' The force of this part of the prayer lies, I suggest, in the way that it is used rather than the literal word-for-word translation. Sometimes we have to be quite careful of literalism because it can end up hiding from us the meanings which are to be found not in the words but in the phrase. The story was told that in the early days of machine translation a computer was set the task to translate some English into Russian. Faced with the phrase 'out of sight, out of mind' the machine produced the Russian for 'invisible idiot'.

We can see too how sometimes it is necessary to translate by paying attention to the way a word or phrase is used. For example, in another aspect of life other than praying, the phrase, "I wonder if you could tell me the time" we would take not to be a disinterested enquiry about our ability to read a clock or watch and whether we would be able to communicate what we read in a way the enquirer could understand. A literal understanding would suggest that as the meaning but it would have missed the point. We take it in practice to be a polite way of saying "tell me the time"; the function determines the meaning more than a word by word literal understanding. Another example can be found in a setting closer to our theme of payer; many people say or sing 'hallelujah' to God as part of their telling God that they are happy about something; strictly speaking this is a bit odd. A friend of mine used to point out that singing "Hallelujah, Lord, my heart just fills with praise ..." didn't really work as the literal translation would mean that we were inviting God to praise the Lord, "Praise the LORD, Lord ...". However, the point is that the function of the word in such cases is to be offering God praise not exhorting God to "praise the Lord".What started out as a compound word in Hebrew "Hallelu Yah" roughly meaning "Praise Yahweh" has mutated through coming into a language that doesn't understand the original words and simply been taken on as a religious praise term, in some cases functioning as an equivalent to "Hooray".

So let's take this phrase in line with the function it seems to have. There is a Jewish prayer which was almost certainly being used in Jesus's time which begins, ' blessed and hallowed ...'. It seems to me that the way that 'blessed and hallowed' is used indicates both that the 'blessed' and 'hallowed' are being used in parallel; each forming the other's meanings. This kind of parallelism was not at all uncommon in Hebrew prayer. They are also being used, functionally, rather like the 'hallelujah' that was exampled in the previous paragraph: as a way of actually giving praise to God.

To take a further example with some similarity, in the Magnificat, Mary uses the phrase 'and holy is his name' which in the context [praise and exaltation] seems not just an item for praise but a way of voicing the praise; a kind of 'I praise your name' phrase. While it is not identical to 'hallowed be your name', it gives pause for the thought of taking 'holy/hallowed' phrases as ones that may function as 'giving praise and thanks' terms. So, I have taken this phrase in the Lord's Prayer as inviting us to give expression to our praise of God and our thanks to God.

There are some writers who take a fairly literal approach to this part of the prayer and see it as a petition for hallowing God's name and explain its meaning to be a petition that people will reverence God and that God's qualities will be known and respected. I'm less convinced by this simply because it seems to me that this is an implication of the next clause ('your kingdom come...') which already has its parallelism. And since we haven't otherwise had in the prayer a section for praise of God, then it seems to me that taking it to be about praise and thanksgiving is fair and likely, given that a normal pattern of Jewish prayer might encourage us to look for it here.

I am also not intending to make a hard and fast distinction between praise and thanksgiving and have tended to see both kinds of activity as legitimate ways of hallowing God's name. They certainly, in practice, tend to run into one another. Thanks for what God has done usually implies strongly the character of God who did it and the character of God is known in the things that are done. While in a human being it is possible to make distinctions between what we do and what we are, with God there is much less room to do so.

'...*your name.*' When Moses encountered God in the Burning Bush God gave his name not only as 'I am who I am' but also as '... the God of Abraham, ... of Isaac ... and Jacob...'. . Then later in the Moses saga (Exodus 34.5-7) the name is proclaimed by God as: 'The LORD, the LORD, a God merciful and gracious, slow to anger, and abounding in steadfast love and faithfulness, keeping steadfast love for the thousandth generation, forgiving iniquity and transgression and sin, yet by no means clearing the guilty, but visiting the iniquity of the parents upon the children and the children's children, to the third and the fourth generation.' (NRSV)

What it seems we can take from this is that the name is about the qualities of God, the things that are admirable and awe-inspiring and describe something of who God is. To hallow God's name would be to recognize, speak out, be inspired by the qualities of God that we find revealed in scripture, history, nature, life etc. And these qualities are displayed in what God does and so thanksgiving for God's acts is also appropriate.

The name of God is covered in the ten commandments; it is not to be taken in vain. What this gave rise to as time went on, is a situation where whatever pronunciation underlay the Tetragrammaton (i.e. the four Hebrew letters that rendered the divine name: YHWH) is now lost because, in order to avoid taking the name in vain, Jews simply stopped pronouncing it at all and substituted the title 'Adonai' ('Lord') instead. When vowels started to be used in Hebrew texts the vowels for Adonai were inserted into the Tetragrammaton to alert the reader to pronounce it 'Adonai'. So the best guess at pronunciation is Yahweh as it is rendered in the Jerusalem Bible; most other English Bibles use the convention of rendering it as 'the LORD', some have written 'Jehovah', using the tetragrammaton and the vowels for 'Adonai' in one portmanteau word. However, it is only a guess and we do not know how Moses would have pronounced it in terms of vowels. So, we inherit the situation where the name of God as given in the book of Exodus is now not really known and we have to fall back on the notion of name not as a literal label but as a representation in terms we can grasp of who it is that the name stands for. So the Exodus passage and the various namings of God by patriarchs in Genesis help us to develop a notion of the name of God which is more about our recognition of who God is for us than about trying to find a set of consonants and vowels to label God. Any naming of God will be partial and incomplete, we need to use lots of titles and names in order to remind ourselves that God is bigger than all of our attempts at naming and titling.

'Your kingdom come ...'. In many ways this is the heart of the prayer. Following what has been suggested earlier I take the phrase 'Your kingdom come' to be explained and 'meaning rhymed' with 'Your will be done on earth as in heaven'. In fact the prayer at this point can be a good way to begin to explain what God's kingdom is in the Gospels: it is where God's will is done on earth as in heaven. It has a 'now' dimension to it: that God's will should be brought to bear on the here-and-now of our lives and the life of the world. It has also a 'not-yet' dimension too: that God's will may one day be fully realised and not just present in patches, so to speak, but in renewed creation where the whole underlying fabric of reality is transfigured and transformed.

This part of the prayer relates most readily to what most people in our society seem to understand first of all by "prayer" -asking God for things. However we should note that it actually brings us into the kind of praying that proves the most difficult and yet most fulfilling when we take it more seriously than presenting a shopping list of wants to God. Essentially, if we are to pray for God's will to be done, it involves becoming acquainted with what that will might be. Here we are on the edge of intercessory prayer proper and because of that we should note there is a link to listening prayer too. There is an implicit call in this not to simply make a request that seems good to us but to hold a matter consciously before God, not just in the mind but in the heart and with a growing awareness of the various human, natural and divine dimensions involved. This requires an attitude of waiting upon God, searching the scriptures, openness, hearing what others have to say (even those who may not be particularly faithful -God uses all sorts of people and things to communicate) and striving to get inside of God's concern for whatever it is.

To be sure, if we do this then it could well mean that we start to feel more deeply about the issue and more committed to it and so we become emotionally and spiritually involved in it more fully. In that way it is possible that our prayers become tearful in some cases. It is from this perspective we are often going to discover the right way to pray for something. And it may be that our prayer translates into action but that action itself is a seeking to let God's will be made actual through and in our lives as well as through and in our requests.

'Give us today our daily bread.' This follows prayer for the will of God to be done. Praying for God's will to be done involves us in aligning ourselves with God's will and encourages us to be giving ourselves into God's will. In moving from seeking God's will in prayer to asking for God's provision we actually echo Matthew 6.33 'strive first for the kingdom of God and his righteousness, and all these things will be given to you as well', in the prayer, at this point, we have just been striving for God's kingdom in prayer and so now we pray for 'all these things' to be given to us. 'These things' in Matthew 6.33 are food, clothing, the kinds of basic needs. Indeed it could be thought of as praying for what we need in order to remain people who are continuing to pray both in words and deed that God's will may be done. We might even say that if God wants something done and for us

to play a part in doing it, God will have to supply the means, including our own means of life and livelihood.

What has just been written presupposes a wider meaning for 'daily bread' than simply 'baked, yeasted flour dough' and it also takes something of a view on the meaning of 'daily' which has exercised no small amount of discussion the issue being that the word is only found here and it isn't quite clear whether it means 'today' or 'tomorrow'. At the end of it all we are, I believe, left with the idea that we are asking for provision for the very immediate future. That is, just as we are praying 'into the future' as we ask for God's will to be done, so we are asking that we will be provided with what we need for and in the next step that we take into God's future which we are making ours, -or is that into our future which we are taking from God's hand?

I am concerned that we are careful with this aspect of prayer. It would be a tragedy if we allowed it to be co-opted by the prosperity teaching that goes on in some Christian circles and in various parts of the world. By this I mean the kind of teaching that has at various times been characterised as 'name it and claim it' or 'God wants you rich'. As with most bad ideas and like successful lies, there is enough truth in it to carry conviction for those who take it on board. In this case the truths it picks up and uses are that it is God's will that we should be provided for, and that God's world reflects God's will for provision to be be made and God's love and care for humanity. The difficulty is that these true observations are then made out to be inflexible laws, wrested from their context and end up serving human pride and veniality quite apart from the actual will of God. So let's pay some attention to the clause in context.

This clause of the prayer seems to reflect the context of the sermon on the mount in that it follows on from praying for God's will to be done, in this way echoing the teaching about seeking God's priorities first and letting God provide the things we need. But we should also place this in the contexts firstly of scripture where voluntary giving has a big place and a major theme of the gospels is warnings against wealth and accumulation of riches. The second context is one of a world where many faithful Christians have starved to death in famines and have not seen God's provision of food. I would argue that this is because, at least in part (no claims to solve the perennial questions about evil and a God of love here), the promise of provision is set within a context of an ecosystem and social systems that have largely worked in a providing way. However, if corporately we flout too much the will of God in areas touching on environment and social justice, we will find that this will have impacts on provision which will fall disproportionately in the most vulnerable in the world.

So it may seem to certain groups of Christians in affluent societies, that God provides all they need and many of their wants, but the reality is often that they (we) are working the system to our advantage: diverting God's provision meant for answering the prayers of the poor for daily bread to our own use. The fact that 'we' can name it and claim it may be saying more about a privileged position in the global web of trade and power than supernatural aid. We should see this petition in the context of gospel calls to redistribute to the poor. In our global context, praying 'your will be done' in conjunction with 'give us our daily bread' means praying and working for a world where the global systems of production and distribution are fair and sustainable. And it means being prepared to act with restraint with regard to our own desires. Prosperity gospellers should take note of their ecological footprints, and take in the fact that for everyone in the world to live at their level, it would take three to five planet earths. Then they might explain to the rest of us whether they really have faith that God is going to multiply the whole planet like the bread at the feeding of the five thousand.

'Forgive us ... as we forgive ...'. Of course there is some issue here about what words are used: 'debts' or 'sins' and much thinking and discussing of how best to understand the phrases. The Scottish version, for example, of the Lord's prayer uses the phrase 'forgive us our debts as we forgive our debtors'. It seems to me that the basic meaning is clear enough: we are both to ask for forgiveness and to offer forgiveness. It seems strange that the forgiving others aspect of prayer is not more fully represented in liturgies and prayer meetings,

given that it is such a strong strand of the teaching of Christ as we have it presented in the gospels and that it is given place in the Lord's prayer. Along with the deceptiveness of wealth, forgiving others is up there as the most frequent topic of conversation in Christ's teaching as we have it in the gospels. This is surely something we should pay attention to. It is a matter of concern then, how we make sure that this appears in our corporate worship. We need to find ways to encourage ourselves to forgive as well as to be forgiven when we pray together, whether informally or in more formal liturgies.

I'm also interested to note that forgiving comes quite late in the prayer; many of the acronymic prayer outlines and indeed a lot of liturgical praying tend to put confession among the first 'prayer acts'. Jesus seems less keen to do so in this pattern prayer. Perhaps starting with confession is actually an unhelpful thing to do because it positions us far more centrally in praying than perhaps the emphasis on the love, glory and will of God in the prayer requires.

Perhaps the implicit questioning of starting times of prayer with confession is something else we should take more seriously as an implication of the Lord's Prayer order and pattern. Might it be that the psychological and spiritual effect of starting with confession of sin is to make an unhealthy focus on sin and and individual sinner?

'Do not bring us to the time of trial ...'. The view that underlies the ideas, exercises and liturgies in this booklet is that this clause is an invitation for us to recognize our weaknesses as far as we are able and to pray that we may be guided away from situations that 'trial' us in case we fail to stand up under the trial and stray from the path of God's will. It could also be stated positively as committing our ways to God and recognizing that we cannot do God's will in our own strength and by the light of our own eyes. 'Deliverance from evil' recognizes that when we are in situations where we are frail and liable to fall, God may deliver us, restore us to fellowship and re-establish us in right paths.

It may be easier to grasp it if we were to repunctuate the older-modern

24

form like this: 'lead us (not into temptation) and deliver us from evil'. I have taken the view that this largely involves us in committing our ways to God and asking to be led aright and when we do fall into evil to be rescued.

The Spiritual Dynamics of the prayer

As it stands the prayer not only marks out different facets of prayer such as confession or petition, it also has a sequence, an order, which carries some implications and perhaps even surprises when they are considered. The order is constant in both versions that we have of the prayer, and while I would be reluctant to argue that this must be the order that we should follow every time we pray, nevertheless it is the only order we have from Christ and should, I suggest, be taken seriously for that. Here we will try to note the kinds of dynamics that the particular sequencing of the phrases of the Lord's prayer seem to commend to us. In turn this may inform our praying in other contexts and our devising of prayer activities for ourselves and with others.

As finite beings, we need to address and recognise whom we address and to frame ourselves to the communicative task in hand. Given the nature of whom we address in the Lord's prayer, it is little surprise that 'wonder love and praise' are implicit in the opening words; they are an invitation to consider and to contemplate God and to give expression to our sense of awe or gratitude or whatever else of praisefulness we discover as we know ourselves to be in the presence of Holiness and Love. Perhaps the Pentecostal and Charismatic movements have helped the churches to rediscover the importance of doxology as a primary act of prayer as against the foregrounding of petition that certainly I was brought up with and which is still betrayed in the normal restricted usage of the term 'prayer' to mean petitionary prayer. A similar contraction of meaning has in many Christian circles taken place for the term 'worship' which seems to have come to mean 'singing songs of praise' rather than 'a life offered to God in its wholeness'.

For me, the Lord's prayer's different dimensions of praying act as a reminder that prayer involves all these different aspects: acknowledgement of God; praise and thanksgiving, petition and intercession; asking for our needs; confessing and forgiving sin; asking for guidance and protection. We impoverish our spiritual

26

imaginations when we reduce 'prayer' or 'worship' to just one or two of these dimensions.

The Structure of the Lord's prayer recognises and encourages the movement from renewing ones vision of God in an explicit prayerful turning to God, and the awe, praise and thanksgiving that arises very often spontaneously from that turning and envisioning. It is not hard to see here an echo of the psycho-spiritual reality which surely underlies most traditional Jewish prayers -and many Christian ones too- of beginning prayer with thanksgiving and praise: "Blessed are you Lord our God, King of the Ages, for you have ....". So many of such prayers are basically praise and thanks with petitions tacked on. This is a challenge to much Christian prayer in the western world where the petitionary element is clearly primary in practice.

The challenge is particularly to a mindset that feels so keenly our sinfulness that it is recommended to begin praying with confession, or for confession to follow fairly promptly on adoration [ACTS mnemonic prayer]. By the canons of this prayer-flow, the Lord's prayer is out of order: confession doesn't come until quite far on in the Lord's prayer. There are possible reasons of psycho-spiritual dynamics that could lie behind placing confession after hallowing God's name, petitioning for God's will and asking for our needs to be met, and we will look at some a little further on. For the moment let us return to the flow.

In recognising with awe and gratitude who God is -at least in part- we are then in the position to pray the heart of the Lord's prayer: for God's kingdom-will to be expressed into the life of the world. This follows fairly naturally. God's glory is recognised and then the desire that this glory should be given concrete form in the world comes quite naturally from out of that recognition. Some, influenced by Isaiah's vision and reaction to his vision (Isaiah 6), argue that confession of sin is a natural follow-on. However, in Isaiah the recognition of sinfulness is a response also to a prior contemplation of the sorry state of the nation, it is a special kind of happening, not a pattern for regular praying. The real reason, I suggest, for preferring a pattern where confession comes early on is that the pattern of coming to faith in the classical 'four spiritual laws' pattern is taken as normative, and the Isaiah passage is taken up because it seems to support the Four Spiritual Laws approach.

The theology of what I am calling the 'four spiritual laws pattern' wants to affirm that we come to God as sinful creatures and that this sin needs to be cleared away before we can approach God properly in prayer. So first we must confess and receive forgiveness from God. The consequences of this approach, however, are perhaps not what is intended and are undesirable. First of all,the effect is to negate grace and turn repentance into a work we have to do before God will have anything to do with us. The message of grace is that God turns to us first and welcomes us. If the parable of the prodigal son is to be believed, then perhaps our desire to confess sin is overwhelmed by God's desire for our fellowship. If grace really is the predominant motif of God's attitude towards us, sin can wait. If God has dealt with our sin, it does not have to be the first thing we raise when we decide to focus on God. That's not to say it is irrelevant or that God is not concerned with it, merely that it may not be such a big deal to a gracious God who has made provision for it, that we have to start every Godward conversation with it.

There three further reasons why we should be wary of making the four spiritual laws our guide to prayer patterns. The first is that it is only one pattern of coming to faith and its foregrounding is driven by a particular theology. It is not the only pattern of coming to faith that scripture or Christian experience knows. So it is not necessarily a good model in all cases for coming to faith let alone, and this is the second reason, applying it it to something that it was not designed for. It was not designed to be a pattern for regular prayer. Thirdly, in any case, none of the theological or customary reasons should have as much authority over how we approach prayer as the teaching of Jesus himself.

A further unintended consequence of confession-first praying is that is tends to feed an insecurity in relation to God that undermines a confident freedom or boldness in God's presence which is properly underpinned by a radical confidence in God's love. What the constant re-iteration of a pattern of praying says that re-invokes a process of becoming a Christian, is that every time we sin we lose our relationship with God and we have to start out all over again. The insecurity this induces in our relating to God actually nullifies the Gospel. And if all of this sounds like dangerous territory where sin might not be taken seriously enough, then I refer you to Paul's writing in the first half of Romans where he has to deal with the charge that his attitude on grace could encourage sinning; "Should we continue in sin in order that grace may abound?" (Romans 6.1). It appears that Paul had to deal with similar concerns, but concern for sin must not be allowed to overwhelm recognition of grace especially when we pray. Of course the issues are not identical but the attitude of seeing primacy in grace rather than sin is important particularly in this connection.

It is interesting to note also that the net effect of confession-first patterning in prayer is to place us at the centre of our praying as against a start to prayer which focusses on God which makes God the centre. There is in this an interesting and suggestive similarity to the historical Renaissance and Enlightenment move to place human beings at the centre of thought. Now, in a period of history when there are emerging trends towards seeing human beings ecologically and in context and recognising that perhaps the universe isn't all about us, perhaps it is the right time to see the balance restored in our praying.

It is in any case important that confession of failure and wrong is set within a context of recognising the love and acceptance of the person we are confessing to, otherwise it is almost impossible to do and we tend to fall back into self-justification and denial. It is important that we confess sin and offer forgiveness against a background of acknowledging the love of God and the purposes of God. These then give a framework for recognising and being confident to confess our sins.

So we are dealing with a pattern that places the recognition of sin quite far down the order. And perhaps it is as well to note that the section of prayer to do with ourselves does not come until we have placed God and God's agenda first.

And even when we do come to praying for ourselves we do so by first attending to our daily bread. As we have seen previously, this may reflect the pattern of teaching in the sermon on the mount where attention to our own physical needs is placed in the context of seeking Gods kingdom and righteousness first. But perhaps there is also a valuable reflection on the fact of the interconnectedness of praying for our daily bread with others praying the same. Part of the praying for God's will to be done, would involve dealing with the prayers or at least need of others for daily bread. To ask for our daily bread is to ask, implicitly, for a world where such a prayer can be answered for all. God's will and our need are closely linked in this way. God's will includes that all have bread.

Only after praying for our daily bread do we come to issues of forgiveness. There is a logic to this. We have up to this point dealt with how God's will is to be transfused into the life of the world. We now reflect on how we may have blocked that transfusion: how our thoughts words and deeds may have cut against the grain of God's purposes. As we contemplate and assent to a world ever more conformed to God's will it is easy to realise how we have, in actual practice, worked against it. It is time to further realign our will by renouncing rather than justifying or excusing our counter-godliness.
And we cannot renounce our counter-godliness without also renouncing grudge-bearing. We can't have a world where we have the liberty to be forgiven and to start again without granting that same freedom to others, and in practical terms that means forgiving those who are our debtors. It's not that our forgiveness is dependent on the work of forgiving, it's that if we are not forgiving then we have not really entered into the economy of salvation where forgiving is the normal transaction. To live in grace means doing just that: to be giving as we receive; not trying to be a parasite on grace by trying to take without giving. To do so is like trying to breathe without exhaling.

From recognising and renouncing our past wrong and asking for forgiveness (as well as offering it), we move to our future potential for wrong. If we have sinned before it is likely that we will at least suffer the temptations that might lead us into the same kind of thing again. It does seem to be true that habits are formed from the repetition of something in such a way as it becomes the default position. In terms of the brain and nervous system, we reinforce the formation and maintenance of certain neural pathways until certain kinds of events or things automatically trigger a response involving a particular set of perceptions and /or behaviours. That is where we are vulnerable. Our past sin is very often a clue to our future vulnerabilities. The Lord's prayer invites us to contemplate those vulnerabilities and pray into them; to understand them and with God's help to avoid them or to deal with them but without sin.

Practices of Praying.

Having set out some background we can now turn to various ways to pray the prayer. These all come from personal experiment and often have been shared with various groups of people whose informal feedback has in turn shaped the ongoing experiment further. I would like to emphasise the word 'experiment'. There is much still to learn and to try and I would value the feedback and further suggestions through the web pages relating to this booklet. This booklet is an invitation to a conversation. I hope that, in addition to giving further materials that space couldn't be found for in this booklet, the website can make available further ideas, refinements or even understandings to readers and others.

In what follows I have tried to suggest things that should appeal to a wide range of readers. It is worth recalling that there are different kinds of personality and different kinds of learning and even that we can and do change in what we find helpful over time in different phases of life.

So we should be aware that some of these ideas will work for some of us and not for others and then some other ideas will make sense to another set of people. It's probably worth remembering too that what we found difficult to use at one stage of our life, we might find takes on a life of its own for us at another. Some people naturally take to group prayer with plenty of scope for improvising prayers while others prefer to be less chatty and have some well-tried set prayers to make their own. Some people find that involving their body in praying is very helpful whereas others find that they cannot see what the fuss is all about or that it is in fact distracting for them. Some find exercises involving the imagination very helpful while others feel that they may be deficient because their imagination doesn't seem to work that way.

Quite often the church tradition that we find ourselves in -or have even chosen to be in- tends to favour one or two prayer styles over the others. Sometimes they can even be quite disparaging of other styles. However, it is sometimes the case that we have ended up in one tradition when our prayer style might naturally be something other than the one(s) favoured by our tradition. Or it may be the case that as we have grown and developed as a person and as a spiritual being, our capacities for prayer widen or switch around. Therefore, as you look over these ideas, please consider them from the point of view of what might be helpful, if not for you then for people that you know.

One last piece of advice in terms of practicalities. It is immensely helpful to have someone you can go to as regularly as needs be to talk over your spiritual growth and prayer. If you don't already, identify someone who can encourage, ask awkward questions of you in a way that you can take and will be sympathetic to your exploring of prayer in the Lord's Prayer pattern. It may be best to be someone who is at some remove from your own life situation. If you can't identify someone, it may be helpful to contact a retreat centre or a denominational centre where they probably have someone who handles requests for help finding soul friends, spiritual directors, spiritual life coaches or prayer guides.

They will usually want to talk with you to get some idea of what your needs and preferences might be and then talk to people they know who are willing to exercise that kind of ministry and put you in touch with one another.

One of the things they can do is to help us to reflect on what appears to work for us and what 'dead horses' we should not feel obliged to keep flogging. They may also be able to help us identify ways forward or further explorations in our praying which we might otherwise miss if left to our own devices. Often they can suggest things about what our 'prayer style' might be and give us ideas about how to develop in it.

If you hope to talk with them about praying the pattern of the Lord's prayer you might want to give them or lend them this book so that you both 'sing from the same hymn sheet'.

A Lord's Prayer organiser or scrapbook

If the idea of an organiser for your prayer scares you because it seems too organised and tidy and likely to get in the way of a spontaneity that you value and find helpful, then this idea is not for you. Feel no guilt at passing on from this section and looking at some of the other things. On the other hand you may want to mentally note it because at some point in the future you may have changed and it may then make sense to give it a go. To be sure, such an approach probably fits some personalities better than others, and in a similar way, what is covered in this section will appeal to some but maybe not to others. So it is important to feel that not all need be attempted!

Many people have prayer lists; reminders of people or situation that they want to pray for regularly, they may be supplemented by various prayer diaries that mission agencies, aid agencies, dioceses and districts, churches and other groups or individual Christians produce to stimulate and nurture prayer. Often these lists become relatively elaborate by being divided in to days or cycles so that the task of praying is made manageable for people who can only given limited time to focused praying.

The basic idea is to take an organiser (for example a personal organiser ring-binder would work well) or something capable of fulfilling the same functions like a scrapbook or even a set of envelopes and an elastic band. There should be a division or a section for each part of the prayer. There is plenty of flexibility about this and it should be done in such a way as to enable praying without the practicalities getting in the way.

The first section might be labelled 'Our Father in heaven' followed by a section or divider entitled 'Hallowed be your name' -or it may be that you judge it better to combine those two into one section. Then the next 'chapter' would be 'Your Kingdom come...' and so on through all the various clauses of the prayer. It might be the kind of thing that could also be combined with other devotional notes if that is something that is already part of your spiritual discipline.

Over time in each section may be added various passages of scripture or other materials such as quotes or poetry which aid or stimulate your praying and also particular things that you want to use in prayer regularly under each of the headings as appropriate.

Don't feel that you have to be confined, either, to words. The scrapbook idea could be very liberating for some. You could collect pictures, cut out from newspapers or magazines, or photocopied or printed out from web-pages, recommendations for music to be sung or listened to, ideas for 'action prayers' such as prayer stones dropped into a bowl of water, or whatever you have found helpful and want to include for future usage.

That may be clear enough for some readers to get going immediately but others may want a little more detail to help flesh it out, so here are some examples and pointers taken from my own and others' prayer ideas and resources. They will be dealt with in Lord's Prayer order, naturally!I will include ideas and comments and suggestions for developing the ideas further.

Our father in heaven.

In this section you might write things like:
"Slow and slightly deepen your breathing; remember God is all around; remember God loves you ... what do you respond to about God today? ...."
There may be items of music which you keep to hand in the place where you pray and so you might write down music ideas, for example:
'Good Morning Dad' tape, 'Adoramus Te' -Utopia CD.
Or even simply writing down titles and numbers of songs from a song book.

It is likely that you will find phrases or bible verses that are helpful to you, so write them down. For example, I often find it very helpful to keep company with this verse as I begin to pray. "[God] will rejoice over you with gladness, he will renew you in his love; he will exult over you with loud singing" (Zephaniah 3.17b)

I have also found a dynamic translation of the Lord's prayer which is inspiring:
'Eternal Spirit, Earth-maker, Pain-bearer, Life-giver, Source of all that is and that shall be...' (From A New Zealand Prayer Book).
And you might put in items that are non-verbal such as a picture of a child being held in a parent's arms, or a reproduction of an icon, say, of Moses at the Burning Bush.

Questions to help find your own content.
What things help you to remember and get in touch with God's presence?
Who reminds you of God's love for you and why?
What gives you a sense of God's greatness?
What doe the word 'Father' convey to you? Are the associations helpful or a hindrance to you relating to God? -Or a bit of both?
If in answering the previous question you reply 'a bit of both', which associations do you find helpful? Can you use them in some way to put into your scrapbook or organiser at this point?
Are there any scriptures that would help you to open up to God's love and glory?

Hallowed be your name.
I have written down various phrases which help me to recall and recount important things about God that I find inspiring. For example:
'Holy ... joyful ... creative ... faithful ... mighty'
'Rock ... light ... shepherd ... friend ... creator ...'
'The One who sets free ... shakes ... calls ... speaks ... loves ...' (all three sets of phrases come originally from Robert Warren's Affair of the Heart).
There are some scriptures that I find helpful such as:
'Gracious and compassionate, slow to anger, abounding in faithfulness and love, forgiving wickedness, rebellion and sin, yet not leaving the guilty unpunished' (Exodus 34.5-7)

And I have also written things in my own words that capture important things for me:
'By your will all things have their being; I exist because of your grace and loving kindness.'

There are some musical items such as 'Holy is your name' which includes a list of some of God attributes and characteristics ('righteousness and mercy, judgement and grace...'). Also "O Lord our God how majestic is your name ..." and similar songs might be useful.

You could also include photographs of beautiful places -particularly ones you've visited and so have special resonance and memories, or perhaps of people who have inspired you to appreciate better who God is and what God has done.

Questions to help find your own content.
What ways has God met with you that you could use to give a name to God, in a sense? (e.g. 'Lover of my soul' or 'forbearing God' or ... ?)
What have been your most memorable times of praising God?
What made them memorable? What might such times tell you about what you most appreciate about God? How could you use that in your daily prayer?
What scriptural presentations of God help you most appreciate God? Similarly are there any set prayers or hymns or songs that are particularly helpful?
Is there anything that visually helps you to recall your amazement and wonder at God? How could you include that in your scrapbook or organiser?

Your kingdom come ... will be done ...
There are lots of helpful resources relevant to this section since most prayer materials tend to focus on this kind of praying. There are prayer diaries from various agencies, books like Operation World, and also things not produced specifically for prayer but which can easily be used like newspaper pictures or articles.

As mentioned above, it is likely that many people would want pages or subsections for each praying day. If you are using a ring binder or personal organiser this is relatively easy as the sections can be separated by dividers, or if you are using, say, envelopes it is similar. If you were simply using a different page for each section then you may need to divide or mark this section using something like paper clips, so that you could more easily and quickly find the pages that you want to use that particular day.

It may be useful to have space not only to remind of a concern (be it a person or a situation or whatever else) but also to note down what you learn in prayer or matters arising from prayer. So you would write the concern down and then leave several lines before the next topic, space for further developments or reflections. Sometimes it can be useful to have a separate 'to do' list for things that arise from prayer that need further action and so things can then be written down and put to one side for the moment until they can be dealt with later.

Some people have tick boxes next to the space for items they pray for -and I've even seen prayer pages for pocket organisers printed with a tick box beside each prayer request to be ticked when the prayer is answered. I tried to use this but found it unhelpful in practice (though I honour the expectant intent which is what made me try it in the first place). The reason I found it unhelpful is that for so many things, praying is actually 'messier' than ticking boxes for the answers seems to allow for. A prayer evolves over time as situations change and as we come to change our perceptions and God moulds our prayer. So at what point is the prayer answered? Indeed if, in the light of developments the prayer changes fairly radically, has it been answered at all? Of course it has, but not in a way that lends itself to tick boxes. Some of the answer is about listening for God to reshape our prayer so that it really is about God's will being done rather than our limited understanding dictating events (well, trying to, at least).

For example, say I start to pray for my sick granny to get well. As I pray over several days I become aware of how very old she is, how tired she is and how much she is looking forward to meeting her Saviour in heaven. At the same time the doctors supervising her treatment are beginning to say that they can do no more for her than keep her comfortable. My prayer for her evolves in the light of all of this: in faith I come to believe that it is her time to die and begin to pray for her to die well, perhaps understanding her healing to be the one ultimately brought abut by the resurrection of the dead. At what point do I tick the box next to "Granny Dryden to get well"?

Questions and suggestions to help find your own content.
What things are you most looking forward to in heaven?
How might those things be present or made present in this life here-and-now?
Look at some of the things you have collected concerning who God is and what God is like in the previous sections, what might it mean to see, feel or know these things more fully or more often in the life of this world?
Watch or listen to the news, spend a few minutes quietly afterwards asking yourself: what items got your interest and why? What item or items of news, if any, did you sense God might want you to carry in your heart?
Are there any things going on in the world that you think are important that the media seem not to be picking up? Why might this be? What might this mean for your praying?
Write down various words for prayer or that could be used for or in praying, find out what the dictionary definitions are and put those with the words. Try using them as headings or centres for collecting prayers or prayer topics or for sorting them out.

Give us today our daily bread.
I have found it helpful to write the following phrase in my prayer organiser at this point: 'Seek first his kingdom and his righteousness, and all these things will be given to you as well. Therefore do not worry about tomorrow, for tomorrow will worry about itself. Each day has enough trouble of its own.' (Mt 6.33-34). Given what is written above, that will probably be no surprise.

I usually have a short list of things that I'm looking to God to provide. In the past this has included somewhere to live when certain events take place, or a job, or the means to do something that I have felt the stirrings of a call to. The thing is, as far as possible, not to treat the listed items (here or at any other point in the pattern) as simply something to be named and then move on, but to linger with them before God awaiting possible new perspectives, inspirations or cross-fertilisations with other things which God may engineer to bring to your attention.

This part of our praying is the part most susceptible to the 'name it and claim it' temptation and you could find yourself putting pictures of the Porsche you would like to help you believe for God to provide. Needless to say, I think that this might be an abuse of the prayer and of the idea, not to mention of God's grace. More akin to putting God to the test, I fear.

Questions to help find your own content.
What do you think is or are your main calling or vocations at the moment? What do you need in your life to enable you to fulfil the call or vocations?
What are you conscious of that is presented to you as a need but is probably not really?
What have you got in your life that you can truly accept as being from God?
What have you got in your life that might be for the benefit of others?
Is it worth having a section under this heading for things that you become convinced are not 'needs'? Something that might grow into a 'simplification' or 'downsizing' list?

Forgive us ...
I have found it helpful to have various things that act as 'checklists' to measure my life by as an aid to confession of sin. For example it is quite challenging to think over ones life in relation to this passage of scripture.
Love is patient, love is kind. It does not envy, it does not boast, it is not proud. It is not rude, it is not self-seeking, it is not easily angered, it keeps no record of wrongs. Love does not delight in evil but rejoices with the truth. It always protects, always trusts, always hopes,

always perseveres. (1 Cor 13.4-7)

It has also proved useful to develop over time a checklist of areas of life that need to be thought over in respect of sin. Examples might include whether one has treated ones spouse with affection and respect or parents with honour. Other things might include whether there has been Sabbath in your life or whether the balance of work and rest has been tipped too far in one direction or the other. It could also include things like whether we have acted out of a sense of being loved by God or whether we have tried to justify ourselves to God or to other people. There are various checklists in circulation from various sources, keep an eye open for them and add them into the file. These things arise from reflection on our lives and our reading and listening and so we should keep space for things to be added easily. It could be too that we find pictures or music that help us and we should note those too or add photographs or print-outs.

I find it useful also to keep a small collection of confession prayers from liturgical sources -sometimes there is nothing quite so bracing as the general confession from the Book of Common Prayer communion service, for example!

Questions and ideas to help find your own content.
What passages of scripture or other words have helped you in the past to become aware of things needing to be forgiven?
Have you any prayers or scriptures that you have found to be helpful expressions of confession of sin?
Similarly, anything that helps you to 'get it' that you are forgiven?
Think about the previous questions in this section with regard to songs or hymnody or visual images.

... as we forgive.
It may be useful to list those who are nearest and dearest to us since these are the ones most likely to hurt us (just as we are most likely to hurt them). This will serve to remind us of them and how things are between us at that moment which should help us to become alert to any budding resentments or grudges. Sometimes having written

questions such as "What am I angry about?" can help us to identify people whom we need to forgive. This is not the place to go into the processes of forgiving but it might be useful to include passages from books that remind us what forgiveness is and is not and also tips and hints we pick up that help us to let go of grudges and resentments.

Given also that Christ encourages his disciples to see themselves as debtors to God's forgiveness as a way of challenging unforgiveness, it may be an aid to the process of forgiving to record the things that we ourselves have been forgiven both by God and by other people and the kinds of ways that we routinely find people make allowances for about us. It is worth also noting the idea that is often mentioned in counselling that we tend to hate in others what we don't like about ourselves. Perhaps making a note of that idea would also be a useful tool for reflection.

Questions to help find your own content.
Do you have a 'grudge list'? Who is on it? What do you need to do about forgiving the people on it?

Have you a list of things that other people have forgiven you in the past? Might it be helpful to have it as a reference to help you to do likewise?

What things are you most grateful that God has forgiven you? Would it be helpful to have them as a reference to encourage generosity of spirit towards others?

What passages of scripture or stories from elsewhere have you found most encourage you to forgive others?

Who in the last 24 hours has hurt you or diminished you? How did it happen and why did you take it as you did? What need to happen for you to forgive?

What questions might you need to put in your organiser or scrapbook that might best help you to identify, excuse and forgive others?

Make a list of words that relate to forgiving, find some images that seem to speak of it, how do these words or images relate to the task of forgiving others?

A daring or scary question this: is there anything that you feel you need to forgive God for? How do you feel about that question? Why?

Lead us ...

In my version of the scrapbook idea I have a list of areas of weakness under the label 'Lead us not into ...' and then things such as 'pleasing people', 'tiredness'. I could conceive of myself or others putting 'judging by appearances' or 'speaking before listening'. It may be useful in some cases also to note down any strategies or perspectives that you have found to help so that they can be reviewed whilst you are thinking about that area of your life. I also have a section headed 'deliver us from...' and list other things like "misusing energy for trivia rather than significant relationships".

It will probably be helpful to think about these things concretely in the sense of envisaging the situations that, in the normal course of things, you will find yourself in in the coming hours. So it may be useful at this point to have your diary or appointments book to hand or even a copied into your prayer guide. At that 10.30 meeting, Anne Oighin will be present and he always winds you up, how are you going to deal with it? More, how can you honour Christ in it?

Questions and thoughts to help find your own content.
If you come across an advert that particularly 'grabs' you, cut it out (if it's in a newspaper or magazine) and note down what it is that makes it attractive to you and what it seems to be doing to you inwardly.

What kinds of incidents or conversations have, in the past, made you aware of things that you do or say that arise from ungodly impulses that previously you hadn't been aware of? What have these taught you about your susceptibilities to sin? What do these suggest you might need to put into your organiser or scrapbook?

Have you a regular timetable for your days or week? Might it be helpful to copy it out but to mark it out for the particular temptations it might reveal or the susceptibilities it flags up?

It might be a good to share these things with a spiritual director, spiritual-life coach or soul-friend as the scrapbook /organiser /guide becomes a record also of important things in your life with -and sometimes without- God. You could take it along to your sessions with them to remind you what has been happening and to note down any helpful insights.

An Assembly of Shorter Ideas.

This chapter contains several ideas you might want to try out but which take less space to explain. They may be used in conjunction with each other or the ideas in other chapters. As with most of the material in this book, it is really up to you and experimentation is encouraged. Please do consider sharing successful or less successful experiments so that other people can learn from what you try whether you feel you have succeeded or failed. Something that doesn't work for you may be just what someone else needs to see. Some things may come together helpfully in a way that on their own they cannot.

Prayer stones.

Some people enjoy and find helpful the physical-ness of writing their prayer concerns on stones and picking them up (perhaps at random) and holding them while they pray for the person, people or situation. This basic prayer-stones idea could be expanded from simply listing names or situations for concern to doing it for the whole Lord's prayer. To do this would require different piles or dishes or bags of stones for each section of the Lord's prayer. Clearly, the stones need to be smooth and not too big or too small. Use a non-permanent marker if you want to be able to change and recycle the stones easily, otherwise using permanent markers is alright. Markers are probably best to be fine or medium tipped and the likelihood is that overhead projector pens will work well. simply write on each stone an attribute of God or a cause for thanksgiving, a cause for concern, a sin or temptation as appropriate to each section of the prayer. These stones are sorted into different piles, bags or dishes according to which clause of the prayer they are intended to be used for, and can then be selected, usually randomly, as you go through the sections of the prayer. So, when you start, you take a stone from 'Our Father' and use whatever is written on it to inform your prayer. Then move on to the next dish and select a stone to inform your praying 'hallowed be your name', and so on through the whole prayer. Of course you could select all the stones right at the start and simply work through them. You may like to find different coloured stones for different kinds of praying.

Cards

Similar to stones but with more potential for decoration; you could put sticky labels on playing cards with different items for prayer or even prayers on them. This then allows you to have a go at several things. You could set out the cards in a kind of game of patience or simply to shuffle them and pick out a few for prayer. You may like to use several different packs so that the backs are different designs and colours, each different design or colour could stand for a different aspect of the Lord's Prayer or you should use the different suits in that kind of a way: hearts could be used for, say, 'our Father in Heaven hallowed be your name'; spades for 'Your kingdom come ... daily bread'; diamonds for forgiveness matters and clubs for being kept from evil and so forth.

Even more artistically, you could design and print or paint or draw your own cards using postcards or printing out designs onto card and cutting out the individual cards. It may be worth noting that playing cards tend to have rounded edges because this helps them not to become quite so dog-eared quite so soon in handling. The book 'Reclaiming the Sealskin' has a set of cards depicting natural objects for prayer and meditation and may also give further ideas for using cards to pray the Lord's Prayer.

Sticky notes.

It is worth also considering the use of something like sticky notes that can easily be placed on a surface and removed later on, it is possible to buy them in different colours and even shapes, so you could come up with your own colour or shape coding. These might make it possible for you to have, for example, a prayer wall with different sections marked by space and or colour of notes. Having a prayer wall like that might enable you to pray standing up or moving around to some extent, if that was helpful to you.

Computerised

Those who find their personal computer is an aid to prayer might like to build themselves a slide show or a personal web site round the Lord's prayer pattern (even if it is only stored on their own hard drive and not on the web) and include pictures and music as well as words and perhaps even web links to items which can help praying from different parts of the world wide web. There are plenty of prayer web sites which have materials which could be useful.

Walking and Labyrinth

Others find walking and praying quite helpful. So it can be good to find ways to combine a regular walk with the Lord's Prayer. Perhaps certain landmarks or stages on the route can be associated in your own mind with the different stages of the prayer.

Walking a labyrinth is a possible way to pray the Lord's prayer if it is a labyrinth with stations set into it like the one developed for BYFC and found at http://www.embody.co.uk/labyrinth/online.html. On entering or getting ready to enter the labrinth, we can pray 'Our Father' recognise that we are walking the labyrinth in order to relate to God as Father and then walk to the first station which would be 'Hallowed be your name'. There we might have an activity or activities to help us to praise and thank God. A candle might remind us of Moses at the burning bush or we might have a whiteboard to write hallowings of God's name on. From there we might move to the second station, here we could have things that encourage us to recall the world and its needs. Some of the prayer activities we have already mentioned could be used here or others. I would suggest that the next station be at the centre: 'give us today our daily bread', perhaps a hunk of actual bread which we could eat some of and an encouragement to think of what other things we might need from God to continue in the Good Old Way. From the centre we begin to move outward again: confessing sin and forgiving the sins of others at the following station. Again various activities could be used to do this or simply to stand or sit at that point. Then would come the lead us/ deliver us station, perhaps with an activity of binding our hands with a rope or chain and then unbinding them as we reflect on what our susceptibilities are and ask God to help us with them. Then at the end we could pause and say and reflect on the doxology.

This kind of idea can also be used in a building or an outdoors area. It would involve simply having stations, that it stopping points, at different sites in the building or area. In effect it would be a 'stations of the Lord's Prayer' sort of thing, analogous to stations of the Cross.

Praying the pattern with scripture

What is suggested in this section is that the Lord's prayer can itself be used as a means to structure reflection on a passage of scripture and the prayer arising from that reflection. This might be a helpful exercise for a prayer group, home group or cell group. It would be best not to do it as a one-off exercise: like most prayer activities it benefits from being able to become a bit more second-nature and in that way 'natural'. Just as driving is best done by those who have allowed gear-changing, braking etc. to become unconscious competencies.

If we were to find ourselves using a scripture passage such as Mark 7.24-30 -The Faith of a Syro-Phoenician Woman [chosen more or less randomly] as part of our time with God.

From there [Jesus] set out and went away to the region of Tyre. He entered a house and did not want anyone to know he was there. Yet he could not escape notice, but a woman whose little daughter had an unclean spirit immediately heard about him, and she came and bowed down at his feet. Now the woman was a Gentile, of Syro-Phoenician origin. She begged him to cast the demon out of her daughter. He said to her, "Let the children be fed first, for it is not fair to take the children's food and throw it to the dogs." But she answered him, "Sir,even the dogs under the table eat the children's crumbs." Then he said to her, "For saying that, you may go-the demon has left your daughter." So she went home, found the child lying on the bed, and the demon gone.

The idea is to use the pattern of The Lord's Prayer as a kind of filter to pick out parts or aspects of the passage that relate to the various clauses of the Lord's prayer. We might pray the above passage

48

through the pattern of the Lord's prayer in this kind of way.

[Our Father Hallowed be your name]. You are the God of the overlooked and excluded. Thank you that you have not overlooked us or excluded us. We have no claim on you but that you love us: loving God, hallowed be your name.

[*Your kingdom come* ...]. We are reminded of those who feel keenly their lack of claim on your attention ... divorcees whose marriage breakdowns are felt keenly as sin ... people like Debby and Harry ... show them your compassion ... show us how we can help them...

[Give us today our daily bread]. We're conscious that we get so much more than crumbs from you, God. Yet, while we don't need a daughter to be delivered of an evil spirit we do need to go away to be with you and be refreshed, like Jesus sought to do in this passage. Please help us to do that...

[*Forgive us our sins*]. Forgive us for not taking your love for us and commitment to us seriously enough so that we stand far off and don't draw near or share with you the things that are really most important to us. Forgive us too when we give the impression to others that they are not the right kind of people to approach you. Forgive us too for the times when we have not kept secret what should have been kept secret.

[*As we forgive* ...] We forgive those who have not kept our secrets or have exposed us to attentions that we would rather have avoided ... help us to forgive those who have used language of us that we find hurtful ...

[*Save us from the time of trial*]. When the obstacles in the way of our continuing to follow You seem great, help us to persevere -especially in today's session at the day centre ...

Of course this is only one generalised example and -as with much of our praying- it might not always be a brilliant exposition of the text but it does help us to pray the scriptures in such a way as to hold our lives up to the passages. It is an interesting exercise to do with a group perhaps after a bible-study. Of course the participants would need to feel fairly confident at using the pattern or the leaders were fairly competent at leading such a time of prayer and it would require some self discipline so that point scoring over disputed interpretations didn't figure too much.

The Lord's Prayer and Particular Prayer Concerns.

In many ways this section follows from the previous except that it relates the Lord's prayer to particular concerns that we might bring to prayer rather than to a passage of scripture. Say we were concerned for a church-planting project we were part of. If we prayed together using the pattern of the Lord's prayer, it might come out a bit like this (feel free to divide up the phrases between different voices as you hear it in your head).

"Father God; we rejoice to be called your children and to be heirs with Christ of your kingdom. We are glad that you have called us to be co-workers in the work of the gospel. We thank you for guiding us to be looking now to plant a new church in Freshfields. ...

So we ask, dear Father, for your will to be done as we plant this church. We ask for it to become a real blessing to the communities of Freshfields estate ... we ask for people to come to faith through it ... we ask for lives to be enriched through the programmes of childcare, health and welfare that it will act as a focal point for ... we ask that you will help us to work in a spirit of collaboration with other Christians in the area and that they will do so with us ... We ask for good relationships between church and community ...

We are aware that we need all sorts of things for this project to work out right... so we pray for the people who form the team - please keep them from harm and in harmony ... we ask that the last of the funding money will come in quickly ... and we ask for good invitation contacts as we set up the first Alpha course ....

We recognise that we have acted wrongly at some points and we ask you to forgive us in Christ's name ... especially for the way we disrespected some of those who had reservations about what we are doing ... and for our arrogance in dealing with the local authority representatives in May ... We also now declare our forgiving of those who have hurt us as we have gone about our work on this project ... Andy Uthers who publically derided us ... The gang who wrecked the play scheme equipment ...

And now as we face the final phase of setting up the plant, please keep us from slacking too soon and from irritability, help us to keep our balance of rest and work and not to be critical but to continue to encourage one another ..."

Praying an intention..

As an exercise you might like to pick up a 'small' point of prayer and take it through the Lord's prayer pattern. For example praying for a particular friend or member of the family. Alternatively holding them in mind while saying the prayer slowly can be very helpful. The words of the prayer can actually silence the rest of the verbal faculty so that 'behind' the prayer is a kind of still attentiveness to the person or situation. This could in turn be combined with the bodily approach which is explained further on in this book.

The word 'intention' in the heading refers to a Catholic idea of going into a liturgical setting with a particular prayer topic of concern in mind and to pray that liturgy with the concern in mind and to pray it as a kind of sacrifice of time and effort for that topic. The topic or concern is called the intention.

Praying the Lord's Prayer Bodily.

Syrian Monks are known to use prostrations and other bodily movements in their praying. Some have suggested that the practice of these monks may have inspired or influenced the prayer postures of Muslim Salat prayer. One Christian who valued posture in prayer and wrote about it was Isaac of Nineveh and while Isaac did not link these postures specifically to the Lord's prayer, if there is a value in bodily posture in prayer and if the Lord's prayer should be an important part of our prayer lives, then it is worthwhile linking the Lord's prayer to bodily prayer, particularly for those people whose personality leans towards valuing the kinaesthetic.

In this section I will outline a series of postures and gestures that could be used to embody the Lord's prayer. There are a number of potential benefits to praying the prayer bodily. One is that if you are praying verbally alongside the bodily postures and your mind wanders or you lose your train of thought or your place in the prayer, then the position of your body can help you to keep track of where you are. For some people, not using words is a liberation and the body can feel like a very immediate communication. In such cases the prayer of the body can feel very powerful and make connections with quite deep parts of our souls and spirits.

Because of this potentially powerful connection some readers might want to experiment first of all with the postures and gestures individually and away from an explicit prayer setting in order to test out how they feel when performing the action or even to work out what actions work best for them -what is meaningful and what isn't.
These postures and gestures are for guidance only; a jumping off point for your own experimentation. There may be a need to develop your own vocabulary of gesture or to recognise that your gestural heart-prayer leads you to other embodiments.

Our Father in Heaven, hallowed be your name

To start with just stand and recognise that we are in the presence of God and as we feel ready to begin raise hands palms upwards.

In this position we can simply 'name' God and /or pray in praise or thanksgiving or simply stand in an attitude of reverent adoration as our prayer. When ready we can then move onto the next posture.

Your Kingdom come, your will be done on earth as in heaven.

This posture involves putting the hands together in the traditional gesture of entreaty or prayer. As we do so we can call to mind the things that concern us and in our hearts and minds present them to God.

As we come to the end of that phase of prayer we move into the next posture.
Give us today our daily bread.

53

This is a gesture of receiving; as if having something placed into our hands. Perhaps making a kind of bowl shape with the hands or perhaps using the hand-position that many Anglicans use to receive the Eucharistic bread: one hand placed flat over the other both palms facing upwards. In this position we call to mind the things that we need singly and collectively for our life and work within the world. Having done that we move on to the next position.

Forgive us our sins

Here the action is of beating the breast; hand made into a fist and placed over the heart -I suggest that you are not too vigorous is making this gesture! Whether the beating gesture is repeated is a personal decision, though it might be distracting as we call to mind the things that we wish to confess as sins unless it is used for each sin as we acknowledge it.

...as we forgive those who sin against us

Once we have done that, we may then move onto the next position which is a gesture of giving or of openness to others; which befits the idea of extending forgiveness to others. Naturally while in this position we call to mind any whom we feel have hurt or mistreated us and respond appropriately.

Save us from the time of trial...

Having let go of resentments or grudges we then move on to the next gesture in which we cross our hands over our hearts, perhaps with our hands made into fists. This produces a kind of Egyptian mummy position for our arms.

... and deliver us from evil

In this posture we call to mind our vulnerabilities in relation to sin and wandering away from God and we seek God's help and protection as we consider the ways that we are most likely to be tempted over the next few hours. Then we can move our hands/fists away from our body as if breaking bonds that tie our wrists; a gesture of liberation as we pray the next part: "deliver us from evil".

For the kingdom, the power and the glory are yours; now and for ever, amen.

And to close we can raise our arms into the air in a gesture of exultation as we give God the glory.

There is a further variation which could be added to the postures and gestures illustrated above which is a prostration for "your will be done..."

your will be done... possible addition.

 In this posture it is often easiest to start by kneeling upright and then bending forward so that the forehead touches the ground. Then the hands can be placed out in front which can be helpful in keeping balance.

It is a very good posture for praying a sense of dependence on God's will and a desire for God's will not ours to be done. There are some practicalities with it to be borne in mind: it is a position in which the blood tends to go to the head and be rather later returning and so it is probably a good idea not to maintain it for too long. It can also be difficult for blood circulation in the legs. So, if there are a number of things that this posture seems appropriate for, it might be best to move from a kneeling to a prostrate position fairly frequently (but not too quickly!).

It can be interesting and helpful to combine praying bodily with the praying for particular concerns as seen in the last section. It could be that with a series of concerns you could go through the sequence of postures for each concern.

Lifestyle Prayer

The Apostle Paul exhorted his readers to "pray without ceasing" (1 Thessalonians 5.17) and in the fullness of time these words inspired monasticism as a means to attempt to do literally what it said as closely as humanly possible. Clearly it's not an easy command to keep and it becomes pretty impossible if we take it to mean that we have to spend every waking hour in focussed and conscious communion with God. At that level of concentration it becomes impossible whenever we have to give our attention to other things like driving, listening intently to someone else, operating heavy machinery or helping someone to learn something. When we do such things, they require all our attention and we cannot really give our attention explicitly and reasonably fully to God.

In fact the issue is rather like that of using a mobile phone while driving a car. It is illegal in Britain to attempt to do so and the reason is that the attention it requires to hold a phone conversation is attention that is lost from attending to the road and traffic. On the same basis, the attempt to pray whilst driving would constitute a hazard to oneself and other road users. It would be wrong to try to pray in this way while driving and in those other occupations that require our full or nearly full attention. Our duty of care for our neighbour by which we honour God, requires us to give full and proper attention to the task in hand. To attempt to pray ceaselessly in a 'giving God full attention' way is doomed to failure by the logic of needing to give that attention to other things in order to live and interact with others safely and with generosity of heart.

Paul almost certainly did not mean his readers to understand his words in that way but probably, if we take the context as indicative, meant them to pray as much as they could. However, many have taken his words to heart in a different way and perhaps Paul was even getting at making life a prayer rather than making prayer a life. Praying without ceasing could be a bit more do-able if we take it to mean that we do everything for God and from God. This would mean learning to do what we do as an act of worship or intercession or confession or whatever: that would be doing those things for God. It would also mean learning to do things because we believe that they are what God wants us to do, either because they are the subject of commandments or exhortations in scripture, or because we have a sense of calling to them. This is, in fact the same kind of attitude as when we are involved in direct, 'focused', full-attention praying: we seek to respond to God either in terms of general revelation or of more specific leading. Praying ceaselessly, on this understanding, involves applying that principle to the whole of life so that even when we are doing things where we are not directly 'facing' God we are nevertheless doing them 'in God'.

By 'lifestyle prayer' I mean praying with our lives in the sort of way just described. To do this involves us in making times in our life when we pay attention to the overall shape of our living and some of the particular elements of the way we live and attempt to build in habits routines and pre-set decisions that respond to God's general revelation particular leadings. Some people call this process 'making a rule of life'.

A Rule or Way of Life

A rule of life is an aid to self discipline and a means to shape various parts of our life and lifestyle so that we live in a manner more in keeping with our Christian faith and we make sure that things that enable, encourage or resource our spiritual growth are a regular part of how we live. A rule of life is a means for making sure that decisions we take before God are given practical and concrete expression. a Rule of life, if undertaken rightly, is a means for converting living into praying.

Many rules for life start out as a kind of checklist for different facets of our lives, including various categories of spiritual practice. The best are fairly whole-life orientated. Many traditional 'dispersed' orders such as Franciscan Tertiaries, the Community of Aidan and Hilda and so on encourage their members to work out a rule of life as part of the joining process. Someone interested in joining would usually have a spiritual director or soul friend to help them to do this and a checklist of areas that the order or community consider important to address in a rule of life.

So, for example, the Community of Aidan and Hilda asks people to consider the following areas as they discuss their rule of life (CAH use the term 'Way of life' as they consider that 'rule' is an off-putting word nowadays). It's a good, comprehensive, list and so can stand as an example of good practice in way-making.

Life-long learning
Spiritual journey
Rhythm of prayer, work and re-creation
Simplicity of Life
Initiatives in Intercession
Care for Creation
Healing fragmented people and communities
Openness to God's Spirit
Unity
Mission

You can find this way outlined more fully at http://www.aidan.org.uk/ The outworking of some of these areas might be that under the heading 'life-long learning', a community member might have committed themselves to joining a local college course each year and to a programme of reading on particular topics. Under 'rhythm of prayer' they might have agreed with their soul-friend to go through a prayer office each day on the train to work and to keep Saturday strictly as a day off. Under 'care for creation' they might have agreed to make sure they compost their kitchen waste, fit low power light bulbs and put timers on their TV plugs so that even if on stand-by they are turned off while people are asleep. And so on.

Avoiding the pitfall
Let's remember that the aim of setting up a rule or way in this instance is to enable us to pray the Lord's Prayer with our lifestyle and this aim is set within the context of or growing our relationship with God and

deepening our love of neighbour and creation and increasing our capacity to serve God within the world. Any system that we might impose on ourselves, even though it is done with the aim of spiritual and personal growth, can become a stumbling block.

We should recall the example of some of the Pharisees that Jesus encountered. Now, the Pharisees had a lot of good things going for them, and on some occasions Jesus commended Pharisees. The Pharisees were zealous for God and the things of God, so much so that they set up systems of rules and regulations for themselves to follow in order to make sure that they kept the Law of Moses and kept as far as possible away from circumstances which might have made them more susceptible to breaking any of the six hundred and thirteen commandments of the Torah. They actually acted in a way, when you look carefully at who they were and how they went about things, that many Christians today would think commendable: showing seriousness and earnestness.

And that's our warning; it all too easy for us to find that over time the devices, systems and good ideas we put in place to help us to serve God and neighbour, can become ends in themselves so that we serve them rather than having them serve our purposes and welfare under God. Subtly and slowly the rule that we make to keep us from an occasion of sin becomes absolute and somehow divorced from its original purpose and also becomes a marker of the kind of proper and serious attitude that a congregation or denomination wants to make normal. From there is is an easy slide into judging people for not committing themselves to that rule and to judging outsiders as somehow beyond redemption or close to being beyond it. Whatever examples I give will no doubt tread on some people's toes but I will hazard a few.

Take the issue of alcohol and the temperance movement. Temperance was not just a Christian movement but a response to the conditions that many saw in industrial cities in the Victorian period where alcohol was a cheap escape from appalling conditions of squalor. Temperance was one response of demonstrating that a sober life was possible and a way to better conditions for ones family and society. The problems for Christian discipleship began when the Pledge (not to drink alcohol) became a touchstone of a Christian's soundness and credibility as a Christian and so became enshrined as a denominational discipline. This took place partly through a series of specious reinterpretations of scripture, attempting to show how abstinence from alcohol was, allegedly, the norm for Jesus and the apostles. This set the stage for judgemental attitudes and barriers to faith or at least church involvement for many people who found the temperance approach was not credible to them.

We could look, also, at the attitude in many Christian circles that outlawed dancing. No doubt it was an attitude with its roots in trying to obey the command not to look lustfully at another person or even to avoid occasions for contact with the opposite sex that had the potential to form the basis for sexual liaisons outside of marriage. Again this attitude became divorced from its intent and simply became a prohibition that both marked 'normal' Christian attitudes and a basis for judging others and alienating many who did not find that their experience of dancing led to sin and that it was a fairly innocent pleasure in itself -occasions for sin could just as easily be found in 'licit' activities such as riding a bus or working in an office. Similarly with Christian attitudes to the theatre or cinema.

So, our own rules or ways of life must be held constantly provisional and reviewed often and revised as needed. They must not become an occasion for judging others and they must not become a means of attempted self-righteousness. It is important as part of any rule to build in revision time and some means of accountability to another Christian who has a degree of wisdom and compassion about such things. For many people this is a major area of their discussions with a spiritual director, soul friend or spiritual-life coach.

Towards a Lord's Prayer Rule or Way
Perhaps the most obvious way to use the Lord's prayer to pray with the whole of our lives is to use the clauses as a kind of checklist to point up areas of our lives in which to embody the qualities and

values implied by the prayer. Let's have a look at how that might work out, clause by clause.

Our Father in heaven.
Our guidelines for living need to start with God. There's nothing particularly startling about that statement, but wait; the phrase calls our attention to a handful of other things: corporateness; a call to intimacy, lovedness; and respectfulness.

The 'our' speaks of corporateness: it reminds us that none of us is a Christian alone; in reality we are part of the body of Christ; we have been given gifts, some of which are meant for the building up of the body of Christ. How it is most appropriate for any one person to work this out in their life requires reflection on life circumstances and indeed what gifts we have to offer. By 'gifts' we don't have to think only of a list of spiritual gifts, in this case we could consider ministries, material gifts or simply things like insights.

The 'our' is uttered in a prayer context and so implies that making sure that we make proper opportunities to pray with other is supposed to be part of our rule of life. Sometimes people have difficulties with the idea of praying with others because their experience of it and so often their expectation of it is limited and perhaps limited to ways of corporate prayer that do not suit. Some think that they can only pray with someone else if it is 'Pentecostal' style, or 'Brethren' style or liturgical or Quaker or ... whatever else. Truth be told, it could be any of these, it could be with a big group or a little group, even just one other person. It could be a combination of these or something else entirely. The thing is that while these different ways of praying together are sometimes presented as 'the' way to do it an supported by scripture or tradition, in fact they can all find scriptural support and are found within the traditions of the wider Christian Church. It is probably the case that personality has more to do with what people feel most appropriate than theology. Some personality types take more to one kind of prayer and others to another. Find out what is appropriate for you at the particular stage of life you are at; because it's also not uncommon for people to find that as they move through life stages, the things that suit them in terms of ways of praying, singly or together with other, change

In short; 'Our' implies that we are intentional about praying with others and developing a quality of relationship that fosters the sharing of gifts in the body of Christ. Our rule or way of life should reflect corporateness and tell us as a general rule how often and in what ways we will aim to meet with other Christians.

'Father' speaks of intimacy and so invites us to consider how we live in the light of developing intimacy with God. There are some important things that go along with the recognition of the implied call to intimacy. That main one is that we do order our lives in such a way as to make time for a relationship with God to be developed. It is true that God is everywhere and everywhen and that we can relate to God in any and every circumstance. However, it not equally true that just because we can, we will. As with any relationship, it is easy for availability to become taken for granted and somehow never realised as we pass from one thing to another and go after new experiences and occurrences. a relationship can suffer death by a thousand 'laters'. So it is with relating to God. The truth of the matter is that unless we invest quality time in a relationship, that is unless we are prepared to give it time in a way that allows the time we spend to have significant impact in our lives, we will tend to lose the relationship in practice. It will thin out and become insubstantial, it will not have transformative potential or the ability to bring joy, peace or comfort, let alone hold us in times of trouble or difficulty. In fact the experience of most people is that by giving focused time to a relationship they make more of the relationship's availability at other times too.

Therefore we can see the word 'Father' as an implied call to intimacy; to sharing with God what is important to us. In turn, that call involves spending quality time with God; time when we are not doing anything else, just developing our relationship with God. The more regular that is the better. Many people make a rule of giving such time to focused relating to God daily. Others vary that in different ways. Whichever way it seems wise in your situation to work out the call to intimacy, it should be reflected in a rule or way of life that makes space for it, that is intentional about developing it.

'Lovedness' is about our being loved by God and finding our security and a sure basis for our identity in that being loved. There is a certain naturalness to us human beings looking to others to find affirmation and a sense of identity. It is not a big leap, either, for us to look to things to convey to others things that we want them to see and admire or respect and so gain a sense of respect and admiration by our association with or our command of those things. It is then also possible for us to succumb to the temptation to use other people as things in this way. Being loved by God is what gives us ultimate value and status. Becoming secure in God's love for us, being confident that God loves us and that God's love is the most important 'thing' about us shapes our life. It begins to undercut the drives to prove our worth by possessions, status or association. A lifestyle or way of life based on lovedness is likely to be one marked increasingly by simplicity and disregard to for status or wealth. Our general rules for living might, then, consciously embody our desire to grow in our sense of God-lovedness by removing status symbols particularly in areas which seem to be rivalling attachment to God, which are becoming idols, siphoning off devotion to God.

'Father' also carries something of respect which is intensified by the phrase 'in heaven'. 'Heavenly Father' as some people put it, recalls us to forming our life with respect to God. This seems to be not so far from the idea of living towards heaven in the sense of seeing our lives against eternity, making decisions and setting priorities which are formed by the sense of building on what will last for ever rather than on what is for this life only.

A God-respecting life would be one that did not bring God into disrepute. That our way of living would actually bring others to ' see your good works and give glory to your Father in heaven.' (Matthew 5.16). If intimacy is one aspect, an inward aspect, then this is perhaps the outward aspect; the face of the relationship with God that others may see: the living of a life with respect to God. Of course the danger is that when we start to consider how our spiritual life looks to others, we can run into hypocrisy in the sense that the temptation subtly creeps in to 'perform', to do things for the applause, respect or admiration of others. I would like to suggest that the antidotes to this need to be built into our lives. One antidote is regular self examination and the other is to do so from time to time with a trusted other person. To make yourself accountable to someone else whom you can trust loves and respects you and does so enough to tell you that you do appear to be slipping into that particular hypocrisy. For many people this is part of the role that they expect of a spiritual director, soul friend or spiritual-life coach. For other people it may be done by one or more friends or relatives.

Hallowed be your name.

The praise, exaltation, of God, the sense of wonder before God and of the awe-inspiring otherness of who God is need to be cultivated. More, this phrase challenges us to ask ourselves how we hallow God's name in our lifestyles, decision-making and tasks. Clearly it should include speaking well of God to other people but it is more than that.

There is potentially a cultural dimension. Some of us live in social circumstances where not mentioning things that we appreciate is normal and where there may even be a trend towards cynicism and knocking things. It is very easy for this to become habit and begin to affect our relating to God. Then God becomes a commonplace in the wrong sort of way and we cease to appreciate God's goodness, mercy, grace, and so on. Building in time in our life to appreciate the Good, the beautiful and the truthful is important. Paul wrote "whatever is true, whatever is honourable, whatever is just, whatever is pure, whatever is pleasing, whatever is commendable, if there is any excellence and if there is anything worthy of praise, think about these things." There is a link between appreciating things for their excellence and appreciating God. We understand God, in as far as we do, by analogy and/or difference from things in our experience. In appreciating good things in life and experience we are laying a foundation both to appreciate God better and to become more grateful people which in turn helps us to develop character more marked by humility and wonder. I would suggest then, that it is important to build into our routines activities that enable us to grow in our ability to think and appreciate noble and excellent things. For some this might mean making time for painting or writing poetry, for others perhaps going to the theatre or football or a concert. Others may find walking hills or running part of cultivating appreciation.

We might consider too how we specifically grow our appreciation of God. This will mean taking notice of what actually does specifically build up our appreciation of God in any particular phase of our life. Fairly basic for most is likely to be the study of scripture, either 'straight' or with study aids such as Bible reading notes or commentaries or discussions or some combination of such things. For some people, reading biographies of notable Christians is an appreciation-building activity as they see how God acts in their lives and how they are changed by God's grace. Other people find contemplation of nature helpful. For some people more serious study of theology is appropriate while for others simply being with others who are worshipping with them is vital. Once the appreciation-builders are identified, we need then to turn them into regular parts of our lives. How regular will depend on factors to do with our personalities, circumstances and the availabilities of opportunities.

Your Kingdom come ...

Our world is constantly changing and developing: chaos is turning into order and back again, matter and energy are cycling and recycling. God has purposes in all of this and we are called to co-operate with those purposes; to be created co-creators; priests of creation. At the heart of our spirituality, our willed lifestyles as we seek to direct them before God and with God, is God's kingdom. That is to say God's will being outworked into the changes and developments of life on this planet and in this universe with us co-operating.

Part of praying 'your kingdom come' with our lives is to be aware of the ways that God weaves the divine purposes into the ebb and flow of order and chaos in existence. How do we co-operate with God's designs? In the light of what I wrote in the section on the dynamics of the prayer in relation to daily bread, it will be no surprise that I suggest what I am about to suggest. Co-operating with God's purposes means trying to order our lives well in relation to the themes of peace, justice and the integrity of creation. We know that these are things that God wants and we know that they serve the needs of our neighbours and so are part of loving them.

Therefore I want to propose that to pray this part of the prayer with our lifestyles, we need to be doing a handful of basic things. The first thing is informing ourselves of the issues of peace, justice and the integrity of creation in our communities, cities, nations and in the global community. We need to do this if we are then to make good decisions about appropriate ways for us to respond to the issues and indeed where and how to start. We may find that it is necessary to take a gradual approach to some things because the changes they would involve to our lives and the impacts on obligations we already have are such that to do something all at once would mean that we did wrong by other people.

It is helpful also to find other people who are concerned about the same sorts of issues whose experience and wisdom we can share and whose support can ease us through the inevitable difficulties in doing some of the things we may feel are appropriate.

Then there is the actual doing of the things we identify as part of our response to the divine calls to do justice, seek peace and respect all that God has made. I want to suggest that as good 'world Christians' and global citizens we should consider making sure that our way or rule of life considers the following under the heading of 'kingdom come'.

Here are some suggestions, then, of how we might consider making justice, peace and the integrity of creation part of our life's prayer. We might start to introduce more fairly traded goods into our regular purchasing habits, start with something like tea and coffee and begin to find out more and add further items as we consolidate each item into our regular routines. We might decide to be part of Amnesty

International's campaigns, or we might feel that being part of something like the United Nations Association is appropriate. We should certainly consider how also to reduce our ecological footprint which is an issue that makes an impact on justice and peace as well as the environment. This website is a good place to start: http://www.earthday.net/footprint/index.asp# . Some people in order to live more justly and environmentally, have altered their diet to include more locally produced fresh food and less meat, or even no meat normally. It is good to find out about clothes produced by labour working under fair and healthy conditions and to avoid sweatshop produced garments and shoes. It is good to consider transport and where we live as part of our response to global warming, not to mention how our homes are heated or cooled and lit. If we take actions that lead in the direction of greater justice and fairness in the world and also are environmentally friendly, we are also contributing to a more peaceful world by reducing the potential points of conflict.

Also we might take in God's will 'that everyone may be saved and come to a knowledge of the truth' (1 Timothy 2.4) and think about our support for evangelistic and other mission work as appropriate to our situations and our personalities and gifts. I know that there is a lot written and talked about evangelism and I won't add to it here except to say that perhaps, thinking lifestyle, we should take on board the fact that Christians tend to end up with no significant relationships with others who don't share our faith. Perhaps we should be making it our rule to do things regularly that are not church-related and involve us in other people's lives to some extent.

Implied in working out God's will into our lifestyle is the need to increase our understanding of God and the world. Therefore I suggest that our way-rule should normally deal with study. Many rules do put study as part of their recommended aspects and the reasons are generally related to the kind of concern that places study here in this reflection on praying with our lives.

In the changing world we live in we are called to respond Christianly to the changes, and to do so requires that we do our best to understand both the world and our faith. If we do not understand, we will either fail to change as we should or respond in ways that are less than adequate. Prayerful reflection and study are therefore essential aspects of remaining faithful in a changing world.

There are a number of ways that this study may be carried on according to our gifts, callings and interests. Our diversity of circumstances, interests and backgrounds are part of God's gift to the church, to each other, so that our understanding of God, God's ways and the world can be enriched and continue to grow without each of us having to know or learn everything.

We need to study to grow in our understanding of who God is and how God acts. This may involve study of scripture, of doctrinal issues, of history or philosophical matters or some combination of those things. Our growth in understanding the world may involve making sure that we are informed about current affairs, history, social and cultural matters, scientific developments and so on, according to our abilities and interests. God has given us minds and understandings and we need to use them to be able to more fully understand what God's will is and so pray and live more and more faithfully. What kind of study and how often are all things that our way of life, our rule, should address.

It is also important to consider silence: of being silent before God. There are a good many books written commending us to silence, contemplation and meditation. I will not seek to go over their messages and work here. However, I would like to commend building time for silence into the Rule or the way. The cultivation of silence has a positive role in refashioning our inner world towards God and away from both our inner drives and compulsions and also from being fashioned by the world; the world being, in this context, human society with its preoccupations which all too often in our experience pull us away from God.

Give us today our daily bread
It is legitimate for us to look for our needs to be met but to pray this with our lives we will need to reflect on our lifestyles in the context

of a global picture. It may be that for us westerners, our rule of life, as it impinges on this clause of the prayer, may be more marked by making distinctions between wants and needs and how we answer the prayers of others for their daily bread. Our way-rule may need to include some kind of statement or position about voluntary redistribution of our wealth. This is honouring the intent of 'our': it is not 'my' daily bread but 'ours'. The others included in this are the other people who claim this prayer as part of their heritage. If you and I pray for our daily bread, then a lifestyle implication of that is to recognise that some of the people praying for 'our' daily bread may actually need you and me to be part of the answer.

There is also a 'right livelihood' issue lurking behind all of this too. For most of us most of the time, the way that God answers our need for provision is through paid employment, whether our own or that of someone close to us, or in some cases through the taxation of paid employment of strangers brought to us by means of a welfare system. o we do have to ask ourselves whether the means that our support is brought to us reflect God's values and agenda. Our livelihood as means of provision is also a way to pray for God's will. That's not at all to say that only ecclesiastical livelihoods are properly Christian, rather that our livelihoods should be shaped or be becoming shaped by our commitment to God's kingdom and righteousness.

So for westerners in relation to the daily bread clause I would say that using the Lord's prayer as a way of life involves having some kind of commitment to the redistribution of material wealth (particularly our own, since we control that most fully) in global terms and to taking employment and shaping our livelihoods in ways that reflect God's values so that our livelihood is as fit a channel for God to use for our provision as it is possible to make it.

In interesting sidebar to this section arises from noting that a lot of Christians have, historically; interpreted 'daily bread' with reference to the Eucharist. That interpretation may seem a bit fanciful to us. However, many rules do encourage prospective community members to have made a decision as to how often they might take communion, the Franciscan tertiary rule of life, for example, does this. This may seem more important for those whose church background is more Eucharistic and less so for those where it is less emphasised. If it is an important part of your spiritual life and reflection, then do make sure that you think about the place it has in your life. It might be that in addition to a regular Sunday pattern you might feel it is appropriate to consider your weekday involvement in 'breaking bread', after all the Christians in the book of acts seemed to break bread every day, even if there is ambiguity about just how we should understand that phrase, it is suggestive that frequent communion may be appropriate for at least some people in some situations.

Other Christians have spiritualised the notion of daily bread further in relation to the scriptural saying that Jesus picks up from Deuteronomy, that human beings "will not live by bread alone but by every word that comes from the mouth of God", which is presumably part of the reason for Scripture Union to name one of their series of daily notes for Bible reading 'Daily Bread'. Again we might want to use this as our cue for making sure that our rule includes Bible reading and takes in anything that we will use to help us in reading, marking, learning and inwardly digesting scripture.

Forgive ... as we forgive
Probably the most obvious implication of this would be to have some pattern of confession and self-examination as part of a rule. Many rules and ways of life have this as a central, core task. There are a number of ways to approach this, and many are complementary. Some make sure that a time of confession of sin is part of their regular practice and take time weekly or seasonally to have an extended reflection with aids to self-examination. Some make a commitment to do so with a view to audibly naming their sins in the presence of another Christian who might offer advice and reassurance of God's forgiveness and may suggest where restitution is appropriate or what might need more work because of the way it has become part of our lifestyle or normal thinking. For other people, this kind of exercise is an annual thing at, say, Lent, a kind of spring-cleaning supplementary to the regular day-by-day, week-by-week practice of asking God's

forgiveness.

With all of these, the Lord's prayer pattern suggests that we should make sure that we also make space for reflection on our grudge-bearing tendencies and identify our pockets of unforgiveness in order to renounce them and begin, at least, to forgive others.

If we have a rule or a way, it may be as well to build into our confession discipline reflection on the rule or way, so that we can seek forgiveness for our failures. The failures may be failures to keep the rule, but not simply that. They by be failures arising form our way or rule in terms of how we have lived with it. Perhaps we have been proud of it, or have allowed it to become a means of self-righteousness or to avoid the calls of God or the needs of neighbours.

Earlier in the book when we looked at forgiving and being forgiven and the way that they are linked in Jesus's teaching, I tried to put over the idea that the point was that being forgiven by God was really about entering into an 'economy' where grace and generosity were the main drivers rather than costing and payback. So I want to encourage us, at this point, to think about how we generate ways of living and general rules of life that embody generosity and grace rather than indebtedness and payback. By that I mean getting away from the kind of social interactions where we keep count of whether people reciprocate our gifts or our hospitality, you might want to check out Luke 14.12-14.

Lots of rules of life have a section in them concerning hospitality and that is well and good. It is the basis of and based on the medieval monastic ideal as laid down in the Rule of St.Benedict and as such was part of the contribution to western civilisation of the monastic orders. However, in the context of this part of the Lord's Prayer, I would encourage setting hospitality in a broader frame so that it is being offered as an act of grace not calculation or reciprocation. It is one aspect of generosity of which forgiving others is another and various acts such as giving blood or volunteering are others.

We should also recall, when thinking of nurturing acts of generosity within our lifestyle that the don't become acts of degenerosity, that is they don't become a means of self-publicity or attracting admiration. Jesus's words in the Sermon on the Mount warn us to beware of doing our acts of piety so as to be seen (Matthew 6.1ff). If the act is subverted by self-advertisement or whatever, then it has ceased to be generous and so our rule should also, perhaps, specify how we will carry out our acts of generosity in order to make sure that they are done without fuss and drawing attention to us, in that way they may remain generous.

They shouldn't be confused with the kind of 'corporate charity' that a number of companies, firms and corporations go in for nowadays. These do good and I am glad that money and effort for good causes is generated by such 'donations' from business. However they are not to be our model since they are essentially a means of advertising and generating goodwill towards their brand or image. They are not generous in the terms of what we are thinking about here, their end is the benefit of the company by means of releasing some funding or effort to charitable causes, they are a form of advertising or building brand awareness. 'They have their reward in full' by being noticed to be associated with the good cause.

Save us ...

How do we order our lives with our susceptibilities to sin in mind? How do we plan our days bearing in mind the potential for things that will try our commitment to God's agenda sorely? Do we need to avoid certain kinds of shops in order not to end up buying things that we really should not buy? Do we need to have rules in place about spending time with our families so that we do not become so tired that we alienate them by our grumpiness and lack of attention? It may be that we need to make it part of the way we live that we buy food in smaller amounts at more regular intervals to minimise the temptation to over-eat.

I would suggest that this clause requires us to take stock regularly of our lives in order to identify the susceptibilities we have. It is probably best to do this in conjunction with the self-examination so that as we identify patterns of turning away from God's purposes we can also think about the implications of those patterns of un-rightness for changing our pathways through life.

I would also say that this clause commits us to taking seriously a proper rhythm of life, especially the concept of sabbath. By 'sabbath' I don't mean the idea of taking Saturday as a day of rest. I mean the concept of rest itself which is what the word means most fundamentally. This is not to be confused with Sabbatarianism. I do not think that following Christ commits us to a Jewish style Saturday or a free Presbyterian-style Sunday, as it happens. However it does seem to me that we should take seriously the idea of a rhythm of rest and work. When the disciples came back from going about on a mission tour for Jesus, he told them to get some rest and thereby endorsed the need to have a proper rhythm of rest and work. The story of creation in Genesis chapter one points us in the same direction.

It is important to consider this as part of reflecting on living our lives in relation to the clause 'lead us not into temptation but deliver us from evil' because it seems to me that the failure to get the rhythm of work and rest right is actually behind quite a lot of moral lapses and ethically dubious judgements. So I guess my argument here is that if we are going to build being saved from trial and delivered from evil into our way of life, we have to take seriously the issue of a rhythm of life that makes proper and adequate provision for rest.

It is fairly well established that tiredness is a contributory factor in errors of judgement in various activities. It's the reason we have legislation limiting the hours HGV drivers can be on shift, for example. there does seem to be some evidence too that church leaders who are under pressure of and stressed are more likely to have moral lapses. It's not hard to work out why stress (which is partly brought on by or made worse by lack of proper rest) should be a moral issue.

Under stress we are less able to control our reactions and responses graciously, it takes more effort for us to do things in ways that give proper consideration to the feelings and perspectives of others. We find it all too easy to be selfish, inconsiderate and venial. We may further compromise our judgement-making facilities in trying to deal with stress and over-tiredness by the use of alcohol or recreations that 'take our minds of it', some of which might be morally dubious. Furthermore, because we may be acting inconsiderately towards others we may be making it harder for others to challenge us or to hold us accountable or for ourselves to hear the challenge which is more likely to be perceived as a threat and so pushed away and the concerning behaviour or attitude excused or justified.

Therefore, if we are praying with our lips "Save me from the time of trial..." but living with our lives in a way that is unbalanced with regard to a good and healthy rhythm of rest and work, we are actually a walking contradiction. Part of praying "deliver us from evil" with our life is to be paying proper attention to our recuperation and re-creation. To do otherwise seems perilously close to putting God to the test by expecting the angels to save us from our own deliberate risk-taking (see Matthew 4.5-7 for further reflection).

In fact I would argue that we should go further and broaden the concern. For similar reasons of making sure that we are in a position to be following rather than missing the way of God, the paths of God's dream for us, we should also consider our overall health; exercise, diet, relationships, and so forth. Therefore our rules or way of life might do well to include actionable ideas for maintaining a reasonable level of fitness and health both physical and emotional.

I am intrigued too by the use of the words 'debt' in the Scots version of the prayer as a way of talking about sin. If this last section of the prayer is in part about avoiding the occasions of sin, then perhaps we should also be paying attention to the issue of debt in our lifestyle. I don't wish to make a straightforward equation between debt and sin but it is worth noting the effects of debt, especially in a world where 'credit' (which really means the ability to incur more debt) is a major driver of economic activity. We should note that 'credit'/debit financing is really borrowing from the future, mortgaging our old age or our children's working lives. It is also procured mostly at the present expense of the environment and of vulnerable people.

Credit ties us to having to earn certain sums of money until the debt is serviced and in so doing it limits our room for manoeuvre, our availability to God kingdom and righteousness. Of course, we have to balance that with God's provision: a mortgage for a house may be the best way of 'claiming' God's provision for shelter and security, for example. The upshot of considering debt is that we may do well to include in our way of life rules, something about not incurring too much debt and trying to live debt-free in certain areas of our lives. We may also want to consider other forms of finance that help keep money circulating in the local economy such as credit unions or more mutual help such as building societies.

These are just a few ideas which reflect mostly the way that praying the Lord's Prayer as a lifestyle interacts with my concerns for church and world. Your own perspectives and callings will perhaps bring to light other life dimensions to be addressed in living the prayer. Again I would invite you to share perspectives at the website which is interactive to allow such sharing

In the Prayer Meeting

In western society we are heavily influenced by individualism and so it would be very easy for us to miss the fact that the prayer as we usually say it and as it is found in Matthew says 'Our Father...'. In other words it implicitly frames the speaker as part of a society or corporate entity, not an individual. Therefore it is important that we explore more social and corporate ways of praying the prayer and the particular challenges in doing this that we may face as early 21st century western Christians. I would especially like to emphasise this challenge for the men whose subculture in British society at least tends more fully towards individualism and putting up a front that is about not showing weakness and only the most superficial solidarity. Prayer is often a fairly vulnerable activity as a group thing and so something that men may find more challenging to enter into.

It is also more challenging for most western Christians to use the ideas presented in this booklet in group exercises than as an individual, since the participants in group prayer will probably have had many years of praying differently and the habits learnt may be hard to break. However, we should note that most group prayer does actually follow unwritten rules and therefore restructuring them is about modifying rather than having to learn something new.

The usual prayer group focus is on petitionary prayer and so those aspects of praying that are not really about asking God for things tend to be found to be hard, perhaps because people do not feel that they have the conventions to handle them confidently in public -even if public is a small group of people with whom they are relatively familiar. Therefore, if you wish to use the insights and ideas in this booklet with prayer groups, please bear in mind the lack of familiarity that people may have with both the idea of using the Lord's prayer to structure prayer times and with praying in a group using some of the aspects of prayer that it takes us through.

I have noted that groups seem to find it hard to 'hallow the name' so it may be well to think about how to help them with this. I have found it often helps to have a quasi-liturgical approach with a list of admirable divine qualities which can be slowly read out and perhaps a response said our sung after each two or three, perhaps with space for others to add their own once they feel confident of the format. Another way might be to get people to come up with their own list in conversation (paired conversations often work well) and then to invite the resulting attributes and good things to be shared in a plenary and prayerful context.

Many groups already use singing to express praise, and so the judicious use of song may be a help for this phase of praying in some groups. The thing in this case is to make sure that there is an explicit link between the activity of praise through song and working through the pattern of the Lord's Prayer.

There are other possibilities here too: the group could be asked to find or compose divine titles and names, or to come up with things that they admire about God which can then be used in some kind of name-hallowing activity. In fact things could get quite creative: pictures from magazines for a name-hallowing collage, similarly 'borrowing' advertising copy from magazines and newspapers; write your own 'Psalm' and so on.

It may be that, because most groups seem quite used to petitionary prayer as the main focus of their prayer meeting, it is not seen as something that needs much attention. However it is often the case that in reality members of the group have been prying in ways that bring in other aspects of prayer such as confession of praise and a group may want to learn to be more disciplined in keeping to the overall flow of the prayer. So the delicate art of bringing to bear a non-embarrassing discipline may be needed, by mutual consent.

It may require a leader or other group member to gently encourage a change in direction verbally (e.g. an interventions such as "let's deal with that later") or non-verbally (a soft tap on a forearm, for example), or perhaps a debriefing time afterwards when people can own up to and think together about the difficulties and breakthroughs they experienced. It might be that a debriefing session could be helped by someone having kept notes of things that could be discussed. If that is the way that it is done, then I suggest that it be kept as impersonal as possible, that is to say that feedback is given to the group as a whole without naming or specifically identifying individuals unless that person themselves is happy to be identified. It will be much easier if the whole thing is approached in any case with the explicit proviso that it may be hard and take some time to unlearn old habits of prayer and learn some new ones.

Praying about daily bread is a potential source of embarrassment for some or a covert way of showing-off for others or even a means of manipulation for yet others. Therefore we need to be sensitive to how this phase of group prayer might be approached. Of course it may vary also according to the comfort-levels of the group with whatever depth of sharing. It may be best simply at first to introduce this phase of praying by inviting participants to mention in a word or a short sentence things that they are conscious of needing wither for themselves or for the church or some other group of which they are part. Sometimes in order to take away the personalised association of a request voiced by the person requesting, which may be difficult or embarrassing in some groups, it may be as well to simply ask people to think in a short time of quiet which the leader or designated person then draws to a close after a suitable interval.

Alternatively writing down something on a piece of paper and pooling the papers for them to be drawn out and shared anonymously wither by a particular person in the group or by each member in turn as the bowl or basket of papers is passed round. Some groups may find the relevant written liturgical prayers from the liturgical prayer section of this book are helpful in handling this phase of praying together. One of the strengths of liturgies of set prayers is that they enable praying together where there may be awkwardnesses or difficulties in extempore prayer.

It may also be necessary to find safe ways to handle asking

forgiveness and forgiving in a group context, the simplest being to give people permission to think things over in silence and to have some kind of general communal response such as saying a confession or singing something appropriate. It may also be helpful to investigate some corporate liturgies of repentance for further ideas. Don't forget to include space for people to at least begin the process of forgiving, as this is something that is not well represented in our traditions and so easily overlooked.

Similarly it may be inappropriate to give too much freedom in the final section on committing our ways to God and avoiding temptation; the potential confessional nature of the content might be frightening and insecure for some people. Here again having set prayers or songs to hand might be helpful, or a judicious use of silent reflection with a designated ending.

Questions for Personal Reflection

The aim here is simply to give a way to develop some of the ideas and perspectives presented in this book in such a way as to make it personal and to take it more deeply. It is likely that not all questions will seem relevant to you in your situation. Simply use any that do seem to grab your attention or pique your curiosity and feel very free to ignore any that don't seem to make sense or just do not grab you. It's not a test, just an aid to learning and growth and if a question doesn't aid, then let it go. You might want to write your answers down or in some cases discuss them with a friend, spiritual director, coach or even in some cases a small group.

Given the connotations of 'Father' in English and the Hebrew 'Abba', we are aiming for a sense of intimacy along with a sense of deep reverence as we pray, and it may require us to do something of both and to examine how we habitually pray: are we reverential pray-ers or intimacy-pray-ers? Do we need to think further about what our answer to that question is? Why is it that we gravitate towards one or other of them? Would it help to redress any imbalance deliberately? What are the trade-offs between intimacy and reverence with God?Is it possible to do both at the same time? If so how does that work?

Remember that what is translating into English as 'Father' is probably the word 'Abba' in Hebrew and Aramaic and that 'Abba' was and is used both where both 'Father' and 'Daddy' would be used in English. Which translation do you feel more at home with and why? Are there times when it has been different? And what made the difference?

Luke's recording of the prayer starts very simply 'Father', whereas Matthew has 'Our Father in Heaven". What does the use or not of 'our' mean to us in our praying? Do we have a sense of solidarity with others Christians when we pray on our own? Is it useful to have such a sense of solidarity? Does the 'our' challenge the individualism of our times and even in many of our worship songs?

For some people, using a word like 'Father' to address God is difficult because of their own personal history and the connotations of the word from their relationship with their own earthly father. Are there other terms that you or they could use which might help them to relate to God that pick out some of the same meanings and connotations of 'Abba'?

In Genesis a number of people encounter God and give a name following that encounter. 'The God who is there', 'The God who sees me', 'The God who heals' and so on. What names might you give to God, in the tradition of these Genesis names, arising from your experience of God?

What names or titles or descriptions of God have spoken to you in the past and have helped to deepen your appreciation of God or your encounter with God? What names are still or currently powerful for you?

Which do you find easiest to do; praise God or thank God? Why?

What does the word 'Kingdom' mean to you in secular speech? Is it a term you are warm towards or not? Why? In religious conversation what do you associate with the word 'kingdom'? What kind of concept or image of God does it convey to you? Is that concept or image useful in your praying or do you tend not to use it?

Lots of people most naturally associate the phrase 'the kingdom of God' or 'the kingdom of heaven' with a future time and state of being. Yet Jesus also talks of it as a present reality in the Gospels. How can we hold together the idea of the kingdom of God as both a present and a future reality?

Do you find the idea of submitting to someone else's will difficult? If so, in what way; what is hard about it? Does it make a difference if it is God? What other ways could we talk about God's kingdom and God's will that might help people who find those words or concepts difficult to grasp or to relate to positively?

Some writers substitute 'kindom' for 'Kingdom' when they write about the things of God. What is your first reaction? What does the word 'kindom' suggest to you? Why do you think they might make that substitution? What are the good things about the substitution? What are its downsides?

If our first loyalty is to the Kingdom of God, how do we relate that loyalty to earthly powers and authorities?

How do we discover what God's will is? What three things could you do or not do that would improve your listening to God? How can you incorporate the answer to that question into your life more fully?

Bread is not a naturally occurring phenomenon; It cannot be picked directly from a tree like fruit or from the ground like vegetables (except in the Land of Oz, of course!) Bread requires to be made from ingredients found in nature and the application of various kinds of work and processing by human beings. What processes are involved? What does bread say about God's provision, given that it requires all this processing?

How do we make sense of asking God to give us our daily bread, seeing as it comes to us by dint of the work of human hands often in exchange for the work of our own hands or minds? In what ways can we see God as the giver of what we ourselves produce?

Does the answer to the last question bear upon the issue of how far we should make provision for our futures and for our children by saving, insurance or investments? In what way can this be reconciled with the idea of bread for today or bread for the immediate future?

The modern form of the Lord's Prayer has 'sins', the Tudor version has 'trespasses' and the Scots version has 'debts'. Look them up in a dictionary or maybe several. Write down the definitions and then think: how do these various translations help us to think of forgiveness? Are there any ways in which they make difficulties in thinking about forgiveness?

What is the best thing about being forgiven? What is the worst thing?

What are your chief difficulties in forgiving other people? How can we best overcome these kinds of difficulties? What things have helped you to forgive others in the past?

What have been the hardest things to forgive? Why?

What is the difference between forgiving and excusing? Is it helpful to make that distinction?

What seem to be your own areas of greatest vulnerability to temptation? How does knowing these weaknesses affect the way that you plan your days?

What patterns of prayer have you used before? What were the good things and the not so good things about each? How might these observations relate to praying the Lord's prayer as a pattern?

In what ways have you used the Lord's prayer as a set prayer?

Have you ever kept a prayer diary or prayer lists? Why did you do so? How did it help your praying? Were there ways in which it became a burden or difficult?

What are the hidden or unspoken rules of the prayer groups that you have been part of? How were prayer times supposed to start and end? How did people know who and whether someone else was to pray next? What kind of language was used? How do these rules compare with normal conversation?

What is your reaction to the slogan 'sudden prayers make God jump'?

If you haven't got someone who acts towards you as a spiritual-life coach, or mentor or spiritual director or a soul friend, what would you look for in such a person? Do you know anyone who fulfils most of your desired qualities?

If you do have a soul-friend, spiritual director, or spiritual-life coach, what do you appreciate about them? How have they helped you? If you have had more than one, think about the contributions each has made to your spiritual journey.

If you have a rule of life, what brought you to have it? What kinds of things does it cover? Why or how did you choose those things? What differences, additions or subtractions would using the Lord's prayer as a rule make?

If you don't have a personal rule of life, is there any particular reason why not? What is challenging about the idea? What seems good about the idea?

What is your experience of set liturgies? What are the positives and the negatives about set liturgical praying?

What is your reaction to the thought that our churches often don't encourage us to think much about forgiving others as much as finding forgiveness ourselves? How do you think we could remedy the situation? Or should we not?

How do you feel about the idea that in corporate or personal worship, we should leave dealing with our sins till later rather than put it near the start of our prayer-time?

Liturgical Lord's praying.

An earlier chapter suggested a way to keep a kind of scrapbook of prayers and thoughts according to the different parts of the Lord's Prayer. Once that is done, you are close to being able to have set liturgies of the Lord's Prayer where seasonal materials could be used and things like daily prayer cycles and lists brought into the pattern. Some of us by temperament or by canonical obedience are committed to praying daily offices which do not well reflect the pattern of the Lord's Prayer. In this section I will suggest some ways that I have found to integrate patterned praying of the Lord's Prayer into such practice.

The term, 'office' in this context is a word for a service which is prayed as part of a duty or routine. It originates from the Latin '*Officium*' which has the meaning of a duty or the performance of a duty. The term grew up in monastic practice where those living by a monastic rule usually had the duty of praying communally and liturgically laid down as part of the rule of their order.

Historical roots

For those less familiar with this way of regular prayer I add a few notes about 'offices of prayer. Early on in the church's history Christians began to meet together to pray together. There is some evidence that one of the patterns was to pray three times a day -using the Lord's prayer. In time communities of monastics would meet together to pray, say or sing Psalms together.

There also arose the practice among non-monastic Christians of meeting together for an evening prayer in which the lighting lamps and songs to the glory and light of Christ was a spectacular part. This was the beginning of what are termed the 'cathedral' offices. These patterns gave rise, in various ways, to the regular, daily prayers that are a feature of 'liturgical' churches where there is a set order of service and usually sequential reading of scripture along with the use of Psalmody and scriptural and early songs called canticles.

The Lord's prayer was incorporated into the monastic and cathedral offices. I wonder what might have happened though if the Lord's prayer pattern had become the mainstay of praying rather than those other developments? Perhaps something like the offices following later in this section would have grown up. In a sense the following offices of the Lord's Prayer are an attempt to reach back beyond some corporate prayer developments to the Lord's prayer yet to do so in a way that takes up some of the good developments from the offices as they have generally developed.

Why pray set prayers?

Now it should be acknowledged that 'office' style -liturgical- praying suits some personalities better than others and fits some times of life better than others. However, I would like to point out some of the benefits of set-prayer liturgical praying for those less used to it. Some people denigrate using set prayers because it takes away the immediacy of relating to God and is suspected of being inauthentic, a sign that one is avoiding a real relationship with God and just babbling words which quickly become rote and meaningless.

Notice that I am using the term 'set-prayers' in preference to 'liturgy'. Liturgy is a patterning of prayer together and can be formal or informal and it can use set prayers or be totally extempore. Quite a lot of prayer together has elements of both. When people talk about liturgy, very often they actually mean the use of set-prayers in an overall framework of a service. It is worth noticing that in practice having a framework is common even in groups or services where there are no set-prayers apparent. It is also noticeable that set-prayers or responses often appear in such circumstances. It is not unusual for Anglican clergy to be invited to help lead and preach at a service in a "non-liturgical" church who will be told that the church in question doesn't have any liturgy so it would be quite okay to do anything they like. However, when specific requests begin to be made about the order of events, it quickly becomes apparent that there are certain unspoken rules for the order of events that have to be obeyed or the congregation will become restless or upset.

Similarly many a 'non-liturgical' assembly will have certain phrases that will be used regularly and often evoke particular responses. I have been in a Pentecostal church where the response "And bless his holy name" was regularly used in response to a certain cue phrase by the leader. I not infrequently find that if the leader of the moment says "And all God's people said,", the congregation will reply "Aymen" (even down to the American pronunciation). In many churches "Alleluia" and "Amen" are said quite often and it becomes quite apparent that there are rules about when they should and should not be said. So the issue is not the use or non-use of set prayers and phrases, but the frequency and whether they are written down or just in people's heads.

One of the objections to set-prayers is expressed in the analogy with human conversation: "You don't talk to your friends or relatives in formal set phrases, so why do it with God?" There are a number of things that are crying out to be said in response to this. One of them is to note that the analogy is incomplete in that it only refers to speaking. Quite often the people who would employ this analogy to dismiss set-prayers are very happy to sing to God. It might be noted that for a lot of people the analogy would actually rule out singing to God since they don't sing to their friends and relatives and the words of a song are nothing if not 'formal set phrases'. So if singing to God is okay then perhaps it isn't so big a step to drop the tune and simply speak chorally to God.

The analogy is also missing some dimensions of human verbal interaction that would be interesting to include in the analogy. In actual fact we often do speak to others, even intimate others, in formal set phrases. We have set phrases for greetings, for showing appreciation, leave-taking, excusing and many of these phrases have proper set responses too. The function of these kinds of phrases is to enable us to interact at points where having to find new words to say each time might be quite taxing. These phrases function to oil the wheels of communication, to keep channels open and maintain a sense of positive connection. That is without also counting in the times when we use set phrases or even whole paragraphs in order to accomplish certain ends. Promises in a wedding can be done informally, but it is better to have a set passage or to have written it down so that everything that should be said is said at the crucial moment. We might even resort to speaking poetry to one another or quoting passages from books or poems because the words say more eloquently what we want to say and the added value of their beauty or the cachet of their cultural resonance makes them more desirable to use in sometimes quite intimate situations.

What I am trying to get over here in these last few paragraphs is that set prayers can be very appropriate and have analogies in human-to-human interactions which we seem to forget. In addition we might recall that God is not another human being and the access God has to our inner thoughts and the ability to read our hearts does mean that we should be wary of applying too literally standards drawn from human interpersonal communication. The real issues is what helps us to relate to God?

People have often found set-prayer liturgies helpful in various circum-stances where the alternatives are much less so. In the same way as some people "don't do breakfast", that is to say that they are not very good at conversation while they are still effectively coming round after sleep, so some people (perhaps the same ones) find that trying to be bright and breezy in prayer is beyond them. At such times a set-prayer office can be a godsend in helping to to keep open channels of communication with God and maintain that sense of positive relating even while feeling unable to contribute much by way of content and yet finding also that silence lapses into day-dreaming.

Some people find they might go through extended periods when they find prayer to be harder than at other times, for them praying an office and joining with liturgical prayer can be a real help in maintaining a sense of positive connection with God and the things of God while they re-orientate themselves and their spiritual life.

Other people feel that they are not eloquent and that words that are well-honed by minds who are good with words and by usage and further reflection are very good at expressing their prayer, particularly with other people. In addition, they may further feel that by using such words in their prayers, they are learning to pray better from those who have written the prayers. Many of us learn to pray in part from those we pray with, written prayers simply extend the 'classroom' to include pray-ers not physically present.

Some would argue also that using tried and tested prayers rescues us from praying theologically inept prayers. I am not so happy with this reason as it seems to denigrate the halting prayers of those new to faith or without 'sufficient' instruction in Christian thinking. I think that God is more honoured by the attempt to pray than worried by the misunderstandings of the pray-er. And let's face it, all of us still have things to learn and it's likely that our ignorance will show up in our praying from time to time. Nevertheless, the positive side of this argument is supportable: set prayers can help us learn to pray.

Using the Lord's prayer with existing offices.
Most 'classical' offices for daily prayer are constructed on a pattern of introductory responses, Psalmody, readings, canticles, Lord's prayer, petitions, closing prayers. Perhaps the easiest thing to do for those who like or are obliged to pray offices, is to simply use a Lord's prayer schema in the petitions section between the canticles and the closing prayers either replacing the recited form or using it to begin or end the schematic form. However, doing so can result in a longer office which may not fit well with other time commitments. The time can sometimes be reduced by using the shorter form of an office. One way to deal with this may be to consider the Canticle as hallowing God's name and a closing collect can often be selected which is appropriate to closing the Lord's prayer. In such a usage it might be good to pick up the idea of using the Lord's prayer to pray through the main passage of scripture used earlier.

In effect, what happens once the Lord's prayer is being more fully prayed as a framework rather than a set prayer within an office, is that the office becomes more obviously divided between a service of the word where Psalmody and reading of Scripture take the central place, and a prayer office where praise, thanksgiving, petition, confession etc. are more central. This division roughly corresponds to a long-standing division between 'monastic offices' which came about to meet the needs of monastic communities to recite the Psalter, and 'Cathedral' offices which came about for the people simply to pray together.

Those with more liberty over what and how they pray might like to consider using the two kinds of office on different occasions: a service of the word in the morning, say, and a Lord's prayer office later in the day.

While preparing *Praying the Pattern*, I came across a daily prayer modelled on the Lord's Prayer pattern produced by the United Reformed Church of Great Britain in a ring-binder file of liturgies called Worship: from the United Reformed Church under the heading 'Daily Worship' and there are some useful prayers and ideas in it. One thing I would not commend about it, though, is the attempt to squeeze a 'monastic' office dimension into it; that is that the compilers have attempted to fit reflection on scripture into the pattern. So under the 'hallowed be your name' section we are encouraged to read a psalm as the main activity, and the only activity envisaged under the heading 'give us today our daily bread' is reading scripture. As I indicated earlier, this is to confuse the task of the Lord's Prayer and it is probably better to hold the task of reading scripture devotionally and liturgically in a different framework. What the URC approach does is, in effect, to remove hallowing the name when Psalms that are not appropriate to that task (arguably the majority) are used and to lose the basis for asking for our own needs to be met because the daily bread section is interpreted in this framework exclusively in terms of reading scripture.

Having stated that, the forgiving of others is represented and the prayer for forgiveness includes a petition to 'help us to forgive others' and is prefaced by an exhortation to 'share his forgiveness'. However, in the liturgies offered in this book, the proportion or weight given to offering forgiveness is greater than in the URC prayer. Given that we have corporately and historically neglected this dimension in liturgy, it is important that we make sure that it is well represented where it is explicitly part of the deal.

Some office prayers.

The following are just a few examples of office of the Lord's Prayer that have evolved as I have sought to put into liturgical form for my own devotions the kinds of concerns discussed in the rest of the booklet.

Most of the prayers are my own, though some of those are drawn from or inspired by various other prayers and writing. They are written as primarily corporate rather than individual devotionals with two or more people envisaged as saying them together. However, they have been prayed by one individual on many occasions and are as capable of that use as any other office.

They are presented as seasonal, either church seasonal or earth-seasonal. This has been done because there is, for many people, a value in both variety and in marking the passing seasons. There is also an 'everyday' office for times that feel less seasonally marked.

Introduction to the Offices

These Lord's Prayer Offices' have, for the most part, been written from scratch having evolved from daily prayers used by the author over several years. The first experimental Lord's prayer offices used borrowings from other liturgies and prayer collections quite extensively. There are a few prayers or phrases at various points that are from other sources and these are credited in the text as far as possible.

In addition to an 'everyday office' I have found the schema for days and seasons used in Celebrating Common Prayer useful and have largely used it here. The system CCP uses is to assign each day of the week a theme from the seasons of the Church's year. So, Sunday has a focus on Resurrection, Monday on Creation and Pentecost, Tuesday on Advent, Wednesday on Incarnation, Thursday on Epiphany, Friday on Lent and Passiontide and Saturday on All Saints and Kingdomtide (the weeks leading up to Advent). The idea of the everyday office is to provide some variation to the seasons/days scheme which can key into other themes that are not represented in that scheme. There is also a 'wintertime' office which uses the theme of darkness and light more thoroughly.

What this also means is that these can be used on a daily basis in those appropriate seasons. It may be that if you use them in that way, you will want to enrich the material presented here. I hope that if you do you will be prepared to share those enrichments with a wider audience through this book's blog-website. The experimental forms with which I started originally had a morning and an evening office. What I have done is to combine these into a single office of the Lord's prayer for each day and for those who wish to use an office to pray twice a day, there is the possibility of using the Offices of reflection on Scripture which are included also at the end of the Lord's Prayer Offices. They can be prayed together, in which case it may work better to start with the Scripture office and then move on to the Lord's prayer.

The offices are written in the plural, so that you will find 'we', 'us and 'our' rather than 'I', 'me' and 'mine' used. It may be that many users will in fact be praying alone, however, the Lord's Prayer itself is constructed in the plural and so these offices reflect that. Many people who pray more conventional offices come to value the first-person plural of the offices as a reminder that prayer is not truly a solitary occupation even if we happen to be alone. It is a reminder that round the world prayer is being offered to God the Father, through the Son in the power of the Spirit in solidarity with all who pray. The offices are written also more as framework than script. That is each has space within them to add extempore prayers or other material and for times of quiet reflection. While they can be read straight through without much of this, the experience is richer if they are used framework-wise.

The textual conventions are that passages in bold are said by all, while words in italics are instructions, comments or source information. Naturally, then, words in ordinary type, in a group situation, are said by one voice, normally the leader or the leader of that section. Of course variations can be tried using different varieties of choral speaking, if desired. Where there are three dots " ... " it indicates a pause for extempore, silent prayer or reflection may be helpful at that point. It may be important in groups to make it clear whether it should be silent prayer or whether people are welcome to chip in.

An everyday office

O Lord open our lips:
and our mouth shall proclaim your praise
Blessed are you merciful and gracious God, you are slow to anger, and abound in love and faithfulness, keeping steadfast love for the thousandth generation, forgiving iniquity and transgression and sin.

or this:

Blessed are you: God who provides, who heals, who is our righteousness, our peace, our banner, God who is there.
Father In heaven:
Hallowed be your name!

...Songs and/or extempore prayers of praise and thanks may be shared here...

The hallowing of your name echo through the universe!
Father, may your will be done:
on earth as in heaven.

Glimpses of heaven be seen today; teach us how your will should be transfused into our world's life. As we pray now

... prayers of petition...

Father, may your will be done: on earth as in heaven.

We seek your kingdom and righteousness, give all things needful to us in our seeking ...

... sharing of needs in silence or aloud...

In our asking for your provision,
Father, may your will be done:
on earth as in heaven.

Give us today the resolve to forgive others: as you forgive us ...

... a moment of silence to respond to this section ...

forgiven and forgiving;
Father, may your will be done:

on earth as in heaven.

Father be with us in all our trials: do not let us fall away from you...

... we think over the coming day...

Guide us O God:
by your light to live
by your grace, forgive
to speak well to all
to act on your call
in storm find your rest
in others, seek their best
Your wisdom to know
Christ's presence to show
Father, may we be, in this world, the leaven
And may your will be done on earth
as it is in heaven.

A dark season office.

*Most suitable for late Autumn and Winter especially in the run-up to Advent
(Kingdomtide) and Advent itself.*

O Lord, open our lips
And our mouth shall proclaim your praise.
Blessèd are you, Sovereign God , judge of all, we give you praise and
glory for the glory of your kingdom lightens the darkness of this
passing age and you show us the light of your glory in the face of
Jesus Christ,
Father in heaven,
Hallowed be your name

praise and thanksgiving, silent or aloud.

You desire the Light of Christ to illumine everyone. May your light
shine on all for whom we pray and chase the shadows from the
situations we are concerned about.

... We bring our concerns for people or events to God, silently or aloud....

Your will be done:
Light and life and love come on earth.

Into the coldness of selfishness and greed bring the warmth of your
loving generosity.

...

Your will be done:
Light and life and love come on earth.

In times of frustration and lack of growth or development, bring the
hope of springtime and redemption.

...

Your will be done:
Light and life and love come on earth.

As we seek to walk in Light, you promise to give what we need.

... sharing of needs, silently or aloud....

Seeking first your righteousness
All things shall be added.

When the shadows we have cast have hidden the light for others,
Father forgive.
We offer the light of forgiveness to others for the shadows that they
have cast on our lives.
Father forgive.

You are the fountain of life;
in your light we see light.
Your word is a lantern to our feet
and a light upon our paths.

Let's call to mind all that today may bring; the anticipated and the
surprising. The pleasant and the painful.

... We reflect on the coming day...

When we are tested by temptation
strengthen us.
When our commitment to your Love is put to trial,
save us.
When evil ensnares us
free us.
For yours is the kingdom, the power and the glory,
now and forever. Amen

Creation and Autumn

You are God and we praise you:
Hallowed be your name!
Blessed are you Earth-maker, bringing form and meaning from raw force and matter, by your goodness we have the means of life; fruit of the earth, and work of human hands and hearts and heads; these are to us the signs of your love.
Blessed be God for ever!

We consider your rhythms of light and darkness, day and night and the sun, moon and stars

...

Your will be done
On earth as in heaven

We consider the waters and atmosphere the hydrosphere and the heavens, the fish and the birds

...

Your will be done
On earth as in heaven

We consider the land and vegetation, animals and people

...

Your will be done
On earth as in heaven

We consider the place of rest and fallowness, of Autumn and Winter

...

Your will be done
On earth as in heaven

Maker of the systems of sustenance, we seek life in harmony with the cycling of creation and your provision for our life's continuing

...

When you open your hand
We are filled with good things

In our disorientation we have dislocated ourselves from the systems of our thriving which you lovingly provide. All-Maker graciously recycle the waste of our sin into a soil for your blessing.

...

God be gracious
Father Forgive.

Generous God, sending rain and sun on righteous and unrighteous, we rejoin your cycle of forgiving

....

God be gracious
Father Forgive.

Let us reflect on the coming hours and day; recalling the expected and recognising the unexpected may befall us.

...

I know the plans I have for you, says the Lord,
God show us your ways.

plans for your welfare and not for harm,
Father help us to trust

to give you a future with hope
Give us courage, give us wisdom to walk humbly with you.

Sundays and Eastertide

Blessèd are you, God, redeemer and life-giver;
to you be glory and praise for ever!
In the beginning, in the formlessness and void you spoke World into being and from the matter of World, made us in your image and likeness. In Christ in the formlessness and void of death you spoke the Word of life, raising your Life from death and including us in his triumph. Caller-into-Being, Life-out-of-death-former,
Father of Eternal livingness,
Hallowed be your name

We ask for God's life-givingness to be known in our world, saying:
Living God:
glorify your name
In this world of sin and death, of blessings and common grace; ...
Living God:
glorify your name.
In our world's global community, in our world's living systems; ...
Living God:
glorify your name.
In your church as we proclaim your new life in thought and word and deed;...
Living God:
glorify your name.
Among all whose lives our lives touch,   friends, colleagues and families; ...
Living God:
glorify your name.
In our laughter, and tears, in our fear and our hope;...
Living God:
glorify your name.
In our needs and weakness in our provision and supply; ...
Living God:
glorify your name.

(rewritten from a prayer in Patterns of Worship, 1995)

God of Life in all its fullness, we come to you in sorrow for our sins, and confess to you our weaknesses and unbelief.

We have lived towards the end of this life alone, failing to set our sights on Resurrection. ...
Merciful God, forgive us.
And restore us to life.

We have laid others in the tomb of our unforgiveness, withholding the word of life. ...
Merciful God, forgive us.
And restore us to life.
Let us attend; Christ breathes upon us the peace and forgiveness of God.

... a moment for quiet reflection on our forgiveness. ...

As we seek to forge a new future living the new life of Christ let us reflect on what the coming hours [and days], may bring, and pause in the face of the unknown ...
When temptation seems to entomb us,
Roll away the stone.
When our values seem tested to destruction
Raise our hopes to new life.
When good and right ways ahead seem closed,
Help us to find your way out.
When we go forward expecting to anoint the dead
Surprise us with your Life.
When we walk along in the old order of sin and death
Walk beside us, remind us of your purposes and reveal yourself to us afresh.
You have created us in Christ for good,
Help us to walk the paths you have prepared for us.

Mondays & Pentecost

Everliving God, the heavens declare your praise and yet cannot contain your glory. As your children, we fly to you: may your name be kept holy in our heartfelt praise.
Blessèd are you, creator God;
to you be glory and praise for ever!

Your Spirit hovered over the waters of creation and overshadowed Mary at the conception of the Christ, and now the Holy Spirit is shared with us assuring us that we are your children and that you delight in us,
Father In heaven:
Hallowed be your name!

...Prayers and/or songs of praise and thanks may be shared here...

Father God, release your Spirit to brood over the formless voids of human society; conflicted and confused by competing and cacophonous voices, drives and devices. Let there be justice, let there be peace and let there be healing

... prayers or biddings relating to this may be added, the leader ending with:

Send forth your Spirit:
And renew the face of the earth.

Everliving Lover of our souls, you draw all people to yourself wooing them Spirit to spirit. We remember before you the work of the gospel as it goes forth and will not return empty ...

... prayers or biddings relating to this may be added, the leader ending with:

Send forth your Spirit:
And renew the face of the earth.

Passionately faithful God; Father and Mother to us; may the eternal flame of your Spirit burn in our souls and warm the lives of those whose lives we touch in person or in prayer.

...prayers or biddings relating to this may be added, the leader ending with

Send forth your Spirit:
And renew the face of the earth.

Be the wind in the sails of our lives and as we are blown forward by
your Spirit may we know your comfort and provision

*...prayers or biddings asking for God's provision may be added here the leader
ending with*

Send forth your Spirit:
And renew the face of the earth.

There have been times when we have quenched your Spirit in our sin
or grudge-bearing   ....
We ask your help so that we might truly repent and know and offer
joyful forgiveness, ...
Send forth your Spirit:
And renew the face of our lives.

Let us attend; Christ breathes upon us the peace and forgiveness of
God.

a moment for quiet reflection on our forgiveness.

Father may your Spirit overshadow us us in all our trials: do not let us
fall away from you...

...Before God, we think over the coming day...

When we are becalmed
blow us forward into your purposes.
If we grow cold towards your kingdom and righteousness,
Rekindle your love in our spirits.
If we find ourselves tested in a dry place,
Water our souls.

In our living of this day:
**yours be the kingdom, the power and the glory, for ever and ever.
Amen.**

Tuesdays & Advent

O Lord, open our lips
And our mouth shall proclaim your praise.
Blessèd are you, God of all creation, our End as our Beginning. In your compassion the dawn from on high breaks upon our darkness in the shadow of death to guide our feet into the ways of peace. Father in heaven:
Hallowed be your name

...Prayers of praise and thanks may be shared here...

Father, may your kingdom come:
Your will be done on earth.

Help us to live in the hope of heaven today; make us ready to do your will on earth.

.... other prayers may be added

Father, may your kingdom come:
Your will be done on earth.

In that Day, death will be no more; mourning and crying and pain will be no more and God will wipe away every tear. Father, hasten the day and in this age give us a foretaste of your kingdom:
Your will be done on earth.

...

In that Day, of the increase of Christ's government and peace there shall be no end. Father, hasten the day and in this age give us a foretaste of your kingdom:
Your will be done on earth.

...

In that Day, your Spirit will fill all things and all shall know you. Father, hasten the day and in this age give us a foretaste of your kingdom:
Your will be done on earth.

...

As we walk the path of your dreams may we know your hand supplying our needs.

... sharing of needs in silence or aloud

In our asking for daily bread,
Father, may your kingdom come:
Your will be done on earth.

Give us this day the courage to forgive others: as you forgive us our trespasses...

a moment of silence to respond to this section ...

in our forgiving and being forgiven,
Father, may your kingdom come:
Your will be done on earth....

As we seek to forge a new future living the new life of Christ let us reflect on what the coming hours [and days], may bring, and pause in the face of the unknown ...

When we are tested by temptation
strengthen us.
When our commitment to your Love is put to trial,
save us.
When evil ensnares us
free us.
For yours is the kingdom, the power and the glory,
now and forever. Amen

Wednesdays & Incarnation

O Lord open our lips:
and our mouth shall proclaim your praise
Blessed are you Everliving Presence, Life-Source, pain-Sharer, Maker
and Holder-in-being of All, Loving God, Father In heaven:
Hallowed be your name!

...Prayers and/or of praise and thanks may be shared here...

Your heavenly will be done in all created beings! Your
commonwealth of peace and freedom sustain our hope and come on
earth.

...

Father, may your will be fleshed out:
on earth as in heaven.

Your will is for the liberation of creation in bondage to decay

...

Father, may your will be be fleshed out:
on earth as in heaven.

Your will is for peace and justice

...

Father, may your will be be fleshed out:
on earth as in heaven.

Your will is for all to come to a knowledge of salvation

...

Father, may your will be be fleshed out:
on earth as in heaven.

With the bread we need for today, feed us
...
We look to you to supply our need. Be our provider and strength.

Father, may your will be be fleshed out:
on earth as in heaven.

Forgiving God, we have held onto privilege and kept our distance.

...

God forgive us
And Let grace live within us

Sharing God; we have resisted your life within us.

...

God forgive us
And Let grace live within us

... There may be silence to reflect on being forgiven....

God who first loved us, help us to love others by forgiving....
God forgive us
And Let grace live within us

There may be silence to reflect on forgiving. After an appropriate interval, words of forgiveness may be said.

As we seek to live embodying the values and commitments of God's just and gentle Rule, let us reflect on what the coming hours [and days], may bring, and pause in the face of the unknown ...

When we are tested by temptation
strengthen us.
When our commitment to your Love is put to trial,
save us.
When evil ensnares us
free us.
For yours is the kingdom, the power and the glory,
now and forever. Amen

Thursdays & Epiphany

O Lord, open our lips
And our mouth shall proclaim your praise.
Blessèd are you, High King of heaven, Hope of the nations,
Fulfilment of the desires of the Ages. Blessed and hallowed be your
name: From the rising of the sun to its setting your name is
proclaimed in all the world. In our hearts the Sun of Righteousness
dawns, in our souls a loving witness is felt, in our minds your
wisdom grows and in our strength gracious service directs.
Father in heaven,
Hallowed be your name

...prayers of praise and thanks may be made...

In a world needing wisdom to read its own stars, faithful God,
glorify your name.

Among those who are excluded, faithful God,
glorify your name.

In the search for meaning and fullness of life, faithful God,
glorify your name.

In the naming and framing of new knowledge, faithful God,
glorify your name.

...other petitions may be made...

As you provide for our needs and equip us to serve you,

...

faithful God,
glorify your name.

As we turn from our sins and turn to Christ this day

....

faithful God,
glorify your name.

As we forgo our claims on others for revenge and recompense for
wrongs

...

faithful God,

glorify your name.

As we seek to be guided by the star of Christ's coming and be faithful
to our baptism, let us reflect on what the coming hours [and days],
may bring, and pause in the face of the unknown .

...

Today into our lives we weave
The ways of God with the air we breathe.
Facing times of trial and stress
We call upon God's power to bless.
When we pass through joyful things
We make to God our thanksgivings.
Everyone whom today we meet
may God through us both touch and greet.
In every task and deed that's done
We weave the the purpose of the Son.

Fridays and Lent

O God, come to our aid:
O Lord, make haste to help us.
Blessèd and hallowed is your name, compassionate, gracious and merciful God, you seek us out in the darkness of our sin, you exchange beauty of reconciliation for the ashes of our rebellion as you come to us with healing in your wings. Father in heaven
Hallowed be your name.

thanks and praise may be shared...

We have been led into a world seemingly deserted of meaning, we pray for those who hunger and thirst for righteousness, they they may be filled

...

Your kingdom come, your will be done:
Let us live by the word that comes from your mouth.

In a world where there is bread enough for all, we bring before you those who do not have and pray for the will and means of supply, globally and locally

...

Your kingdom come, your will be done:
Let us live by the word that comes from your mouth.

In a world of insecurity and danger, we pray for the protection of the vulnerable

...

Your kingdom come, your will be done:
Let us live by the word that comes from your mouth.

In a world of powers and ambition, we pray for those who make decisions affecting the lives of others

...

Your kingdom come, your will be done:
Let us live by the word that comes from your mouth.

seeking first your kingdom & righteousness
May all things needful be added to us.
You open your hand
and satisfy the desires of every living thing.

Prayers for needs may be voiced....

We have not loved you with all our heart, with all our attitudes.
God be gracious;
Lord, have mercy.
We have not loved you with all our soul and mind; with all our decisions
God be gracious;
Lord, have mercy.
We have not loved you with all our strength; with all our lifestyle
God be gracious;
Lord, have mercy
We have not forgiven others; and we repent.
God be gracious;
Lord, have mercy

O Soul be joyful; the loving God stretches out his merciful hand to you.

...

Make us instruments of your peace:
and let your glory be over all the earth.

...pause to reflect on the coming day...

Tempted to breaden stones:
May your Word give us life.
Tested by intimations of invincibility:
Make us wise in your ways.
Trialled by the seductions of power:
Keep us true to you.

Saturdays & Kingdom

O Lord, open our lips
And our mouth shall proclaim your praise.
Blessèd are you, Heaven's High King and judge of all, we give you
praise and honour for   the glory of your kingdom   lightens the
darkness of this passing age and you show us the light of your glory in
the face of Jesus Christ,
Father in heaven,
Hallowed be your name

praise and thanksgiving, silent or aloud.

Your will is for the Light of Christ to illumine everyone. May your
light shine on all for whom we pray and chase the shadows from the
situations we are concerned about.

We bring our concerns for people or events to God, silently or aloud.

In the kingdom of light, death will be no more; mourning and crying
and pain will be no more and God will wipe away every tear. Father,
chase away the shadows of this age, grant us the first fruits of your
will on earth:
Your kingdom Come.

...

In that day, of the increase of Christ's government and peace there
shall be no end. Father, chase away the shadows of this age, grant us
the first fruits of your will on earth:
Your kingdom Come.

...

In that day, your Spirit will fill all things and all shall know you.
Father, chase away the shadows of this age, grant us the first fruits of
your will on earth:
Your kingdom Come.

...

As we seek to walk in Light, you promise to give what we need....

sharing of needs, silently or aloud...

Seeking first your righteousness
All things shall be added.

When the shadows we have cast have hidden the light for others,
Father forgive.
We forgive the shadows others have cast on our lives.
Father forgive.

You are the fountain of life;
in your light we see light.
Your word is a lantern to our feet
and a light upon our paths.

We reflect on the coming day.

In all that today may bring; the anticipated and the surprising. The pleasant and the testing;
Go before us, alert us to the real issues,
strengthen us for Good, awaken us if we sleepwalk into sin,
show us the way out of the Dead-ends
and fill us with love, hope and peace as we cling fast to you.
Amen.

Services of the Word and Reflection on Scripture.

These services are a supplement for those who would also like to experiment with a service of the word in conjunction with the Offices of the Lord's Prayer. There are two basic needs being fulfilled by daily prayer offices; the so-called 'monastic' centred on the reading of scripture and the 'cathedral' office which centres on prayer itself. Most of our set-prayer offices today tend to be monastic in origin but tag on cathedral elements.

The Lord's prayer structure does not lend itself to a scriptural meditation focus and so there is no place in the Lord's Prayer Offices for scripture reading. However, for many people, regular reflection on scripture is important and a liturgical framework may be helpful, so there follows a set of offices that could be used as services of the word. They could be used at a different point in a day to the Lord's Prayer office; e.g. one in the morning and one in the evening, or they could be combined in one sitting; one after the other. The normal form of offices would suggest that the scripture-centred office is first and the prayer office second, but that is totally up to the person praying; what works or not.

The following services of the word are based roughly on the structure of simple morning and evening prayer offices. For the most part they contain canticles, that is scriptural passages thought suitable to follow readings and reflection. These are based on either commonly agreed English language liturgical texts or are taken from the NRSV of the Bible. They are not printed in bold but may be said together or in parts, responsively or antiphonally.

The service that follow are not claimed to be definitive; they are included really as a convenience and a standing invitation to improve them or to adapt them. There are services produced by various churches for use as essentially monastic offices where the prayer component is small. If you wish to use one of these and to add a Lord's Prayer office to them, then I would suggest that after the canticle might be the place to bring in the Lord's Prayer office.

An everyday service of the word.

A Bible may be carried into the worship space and opened.

O God, make speed to save us
O Lord make haste to help us.
Seek the Lord while he may be found,
call upon him while he is near;
let the wicked forsake their way,
and the unrighteous their thoughts;

Psalmody

We do not live by bread alone
but by every word that comes from the mouth of God.

Reading[s]

God's word is very near to us;
it is in our mouths and in our hearts for us to observe

Reflection together, silently and/or aloud.

A Canticle of God's Word.

My thoughts are not your thoughts,
nor are your ways my ways, says the Lord.
For as the heavens are higher than the earth, s
o are my ways higher than your ways and my thoughts than your
thoughts.
For as the rain and the snow come down from heaven,
and do not return there until they have watered the earth,
making it bring forth and sprout, giving seed to the sower and bread to
the eater,
so shall my word be that goes out from my mouth;
it shall not return to me empty,
but it shall accomplish that which I purpose, and succeed in the thing
for which I sent it.
For you shall go out in joy, and be led back in peace;
the mountains and the hills before you shall burst into song,
and all the trees of the field shall clap their hands.

[Isaiah 55.8-12]

May the Grace of our Lord Jesus Christ, the love of God and the fellowship of the Holy Spirit be with us all, now and forever. Amen

The Bible may be closed and/or taken out.

A service for dark seasons

A candle may be lit or carried into the worship space.

In your word, O Light of the World, we live, move and have our
being. As you have lightened our darkness in the past,
we ask, Everliving God, for your awakening within: leading us from
delusion to truth, and unto your righteous way.
Lead us, Source of all Being, Father and Mother to us:
From darkness to light and into your gracious will.
Lead us, Christ, our Friend and our Brother;
From death to eternal life and into your infinite joy;
Lead us, Divine Spirit, empowering Life within
for we seek your enabling touch.

[Based on a prayer from the Church of South India]

Psalmody

Reader: In the beginning God's word was 'Let there be light'
In your light may we see light.

Reading[s]

At the end of the reading[s]:

Your word O Lord, is a lamp to our feet and a light to our path.
Sustain us according to your promise and we shall live.

Reflection together, silently and/or aloud.

A Canticle of Salvation

The people walking in darkness have seen a great light;
on those living in the land of darkness, a light has dawned.
You have enlarged the nation and increased its joy.
The people have rejoiced before You as they rejoice at harvest time
For You have shattered their burdensome yoke and the rod on their
shoulders,the staff of their oppressor,
For a child will be born for us, a son will be given to us,
and the government will be on His shoulders.
He will be named Wonderful Counsellor, Mighty God, Eternal Father,
Prince of Peace.
The dominion will be vast, and its prosperity will never end.
He will reign on the throne of David and over his kingdom,

to establish and sustain it with justice and righteousness from now on and forever.
The zeal of the Lord of Hosts will accomplish this.

[Excerpted from Isaiah 9.2-7]

Father of Lights,
you sent Christ to bring us the light of you glory reflected in his face.
May your justice and mercy dawn for the whole earth.
Give us light to walk by and means to serve you in the coming days.
Take from us our inner shadows as we repent of walking in darkness and as we forgive those who have darkened our lives.
Let your light shine on our paths
so we may guided into the ways of peace,
through Jesus Christ our light and our salvation.
Amen.

(You may note that this latter, collect-style, prayer is patterned according to the Lord's Prayer)

Sundays and Eastertide

Source of all life, as a flower towards the sun:
We turn to you
Saviour of all life, as a child to her mother:
We turn to you.
Sustainer of all life, as music to silence:
We turn to you.

Psalmody:- On Sundays & In Eastertide

Week 1 & Sundays: 118, 117. Week.2 & Mondays:81. Week.3 & Tuesdays: 135..
Week. 4 & Wednesdays: 139. Week. 5 & Thursdays: 33 Week.6 & Fridays 30.
Week .7 & Saturdays: 66

Reader: Let us attend; words of life in *[passage is announced]....*

The reading

Reader: Here ends the reading.
Here begins its outworking.

There may be a time of quiet and/or shared reflection.

Let us declare our faith in the resurrection of our Lord Jesus Christ:
Christ died for our sins in accordance with the sciptures;
he was buried; he was raised to life on the third day
in accordance with the scriptures;
afterwards he appeared to his followers, and to all the apostles:
this we have received, and this we believe. Amen.

After the scriptural declaration of faith, either continue with a Lord's Prayer office or
close with appropriate words or ceremony. It may be appropriate to use a collect
prayer and to say the words of the grace or to use endings from other prayer books.

Mondays & Pentecost

How lovely is your dwelling place O Lord Almighty! My soul longs, even faints for the courts of the Lord. My heart and my flesh cry out for the living God.

Who is it that we seek?
We seek God: Sender, Sent and Sending.
Let's seek God with all our heart
Amen. God be our centre.
Let's seek God with all our soul
Amen. God be our vision.
Let's seek God with all our mind
Amen. God be our wisdom.
Let's seek God with all our strength
Amen. God be our souls' shelter.

Psalmody

Week 1& Sundays: 15, 24. Week. 2 & Mondays: 2, 65.,Week. 3 & Tuesdays: 110 121., Week. 4 & Wednesdays: 8, 99. Week. 5 & Thursdays: 47. Week.6 & Fridays:111, 46. Week. 7 & Saturdays: 29 ,93

God, by your Spirit, move over the face of our hearts and minds to bring light and life. Bring order to our decisions, attitudes and thinking with with the strange attractor of your Wisdom
Reader:, Let us listen for the word of life.

The readings are announced and read

Reader: God has sent forth the word
May it not return empty.

A Song of Ezekiel
I will take you from the nations, and gather you from all the countries,
I will sprinkle clean water upon you,
and you shall be clean from all your uncleannesses,
and from all your idols I will cleanse you.
A new heart I will give you,
and a new spirit I will put within you;
and I will remove from your body the heart of stone

and give you a heart of flesh. you shall be my people, and I will be your God.

[Ezekiel 36.24-26,28b]

Glory to the Father and to the Son and to the Holy Spirit; as it was in the beginning is now and shall be for ever. Amen.

After the canticle either continue with a Lord's Prayer office or close with appropriate words or ceremony. It may be appropriate to use a collect prayer and to say the words of the grace or to use endings from other prayer books.

Tuesdays & Advent

One thing I have asked of the Lord, this is what I seek: that I may
dwell in the house of the Lord all the days of my life;
to behold the beauty of the Lord and to seek God in the temple

Who is it that we seek?
We seek the Alpha and the Omega:
who was and is and is to come.
Let's seek God with all our heart
Amen. God be our centre.
Let's seek God with all our soul
Amen. God be our vision.
Let's seek God with all our mind
Amen. God be our wisdom.
Let's seek God with all our strength
Amen. God be our souls' shelter.

Psalmody

On Tuesdays or In Advent. Week 1 & Sundays: 1, 25, 117. Week.2 & Mondays: 70,
75. Week 3 & Tuesdays: 50, 146. Week .4 & Wednesday:28, 76, 147. 13-end.
Thursdays: 62, 82, Fridays: 40, 147. 1-12. Saturdays: 9, 146

My soul faints with longing for your salvation,
and in your word have I put my hope.

Reading[s]

The word be that goes out from God's mouth shall not return empty,
it shall accomplish God's purpose,
and succeed in what it is sent to do.

reflection silently and/or together out loud.

The Benedictus or The Song of Zechariah
Blessed are you, Lord, the God of Israel;
for you have come to your people and set them free.
You have raised up for us a mighty Saviour,
born of the house of your servant David.
Through your holy prophets you promised of old
to save us from our enemies,

from the hands of all who hate us;
to show mercy to our forebears
and to remember your holy covenant.
This was the oath you swore to our father Abraham:
to set us free from the hands of our enemies,
free to worship you without fear,
holy and righteous before you,
all the days of our life.
And you, child, shall be called the prophet of the Most High,
for you will go before the Lord to prepare the way,
to give God's people knowledge of salvation
by the forgiveness of their sins.
In the tender compassion of our God
the dawn from on high shall break upon us,
to shine on those who dwell in darkness and the shadow of death,
and to guide our feet into the way of peace.

After the canticle either continue with a Lord's Prayer office or close with appropriate words or ceremony. It may be appropriate to use a collect prayer and to say the words of the grace or to use endings from other prayer books.

Wednesdays & Incarnation

O God open our souls
to awaken to your presence
O God open our minds
to hear your call
O God open our hearts
to know your love
O God open our lives
to be fully alive in Christ by the Spirit.

Psalmody

*Week 1: 89. 5-18; 147. 13-end   Week 2: 85, 147. 13-end   Week 3:
112, 147. 13-end Week 4: 19, 147. 13-end   Week 5: 113, 147. 13-end
Week.6: 20, 147. 13-end Week. 7: 9 6, 147. 13-end*

In Christmastide 25 Dec: 19, 97, 117. 26 Dec: 13, 147. 1-12. 27 Dec: 92, 147. 13-
end. 28 Dec: 36, 146, 29. Dec: 20, 149. 30 Dec: 96, 148. 31 Dec: 132, 117. 1 Jan:
148, 150. 2 Jan: 89. 5-18; 146. 3 Jan: 111, 147. 1-12. 4 Jan: 112, 148. 5 Jan: 113,
149

As we hear the scriptures read, may they lead us to the Christ.
And may we find in Jesus the fulfilment of all our searching.

reading[s] & reflection

Blessed are those who hear the word of God
And obey it.

Jesus asks us who we think he is ...
You are the Messiah The Son of the Living God.
**We believe You are the Messiah, the Son of God, who was to
come into the world**

Magnificat (The Song of Mary)
My soul proclaims the greatness of the Lord;
my spirit rejoices in God my Saviour,
for you, Lord, have looked with favour on your lowly servant.
From this day all generations will call me blessed:
you, the Almighty, have done great things for me,

126

and holy is your name.
You have mercy on those who fear you
from generation to generation.
You have shown strength with your arm
and scattered the proud in their conceit,
casting down the mighty from their thrones
and lifting up the lowly.
You have filled the hungry with good things,
and sent the rich away empty.
You have come to the aid of your servant Israel,
to remember your promise of mercy,
the promise made to our forebears,
to Abraham and his children forever.

English translation of the Magnificat -The Song of Mary, Luke 1:46-55-
copyright © 1988, by the English Language Liturgical Consultation.
Used by permission.

After the canticle either continue with a Lord's Prayer office or close with
appropriate words or ceremony. It may be appropriate to use a collect prayer and to
say the words of the grace or to use endings from other prayer books.

Thursdays & Epiphany

In your word, O Light of the World, we live, move and have our being. As you have lightened the darkness of many in the past, we ask, Everliving God, for your awakening within: leading us from delusion to truth, and unto your righteous way.
Lead us, Source of all Being, Father and Mother to us:
From darkness to light and into your gracious will.
Lead us, Christ, our Friend and our Brother;
From death to eternal life and into your infinite joy;
Lead us, Divine Spirit, empowering Life within
for we seek your enabling touch.

[Based on a prayer from the Church of South India]

Psalmody

Week 1 & Sunday: 93. Week. 2 & Monday: 99. Week 3 & Tuesday: 97. Week 4 & Wednesday: 66. Week 5 & Thursday: 24. Week 6 & Friday: 57. Week 7 & Saturday: 21

As we hear the scriptures read, may they lead us to the Christ.
And may we find in Jesus the fulfilment of all our searching.

reading[s] & reflection

Blessed are those who hear the word of God
And obey it.

Jesus call us to continue to follow him.

... silence for reflection...

Lord Christ Jesus, we hear your call.
To whom shall we go? You have the words of eternal life. We believe and know that you are the Holy One of God.

Nunc dimittis (The Song of Simeon)
Now, Lord, you let your servant go in peace:
your word has been fulfilled.
My own eyes have seen the salvation
which you have prepared in the sight of every people:
a light to reveal you to the nations

and the glory of your people Israel.

Glory to the Father and to the Son and to the Holy Spirit; as it was in the beginning is now and shall be for ever. Amen.

After the canticle either continue with a Lord's Prayer office or close with appropriate words or ceremony. It may be appropriate to use a collect prayer and to say the words of the grace or to use endings from other prayer books.

Fridays & Lent

As the deer pants for streams of water,
so my soul longs after you, O god.
My soul thirsts for God, for the living God.

Who is it that we seek?
We seek God: gracious and compassionate
Let's seek with all our heart
Amen. God be our centre.
Let's seek with all our soul
Amen. God be our vision.
Let's seek with all our mind
Amen. God be our wisdom.
Let's seek with all our strength
Amen. God be our souls' shelter.

On the cross, Jesus spoke words from scripture,
tempted in the desert Jesus resisted with words of scripture.
May we learn and inwardly digest the message from God we hear.

Psalmody

Fridays: Week 1:26, Week 2: 32, Week 3: 56. Week 4:3, 6. Week 5: 25. Week 6: 39. Week 7: 13, 124.
Lent: Sunday: Monday: 26. Tuesday: 32. Wednesday: 3, 6. Thursday: 25. Friday: 39. Saturday: 13, 124, 49

Passiontide: Sunday: 20, 122. Monday: 73. Tuesday: 35. Wednesday: 55. Thursday: 40, 54. Friday: 69. Saturday: 23, 88.

Reading[s].

Jesus call us to faith in Him.

.... silence for reflection...

Lord, we believe,
help us in our unbelief.

The Beatitudes
Blessed are the poor in spirit,

for theirs is the kingdom of heaven.
Blessed are those who mourn,
for they will be comforted.
Blessed are the meek,
for they will inherit the earth.
Blessed are those who hunger and thirst for righteousness,
for they will be filled.
Blessed are the merciful,
for they will receive mercy.
Blessed are the pure in heart,
for they will see God.
Blessed are the peacemakers,
for they will be called children of God.
Blessed are those who are persecuted for righteousness' sake,
for theirs is the kingdom of heaven.
Glory . . .

Matthew 5:3-12 (NRSV)

After the canticle either continue with a Lord's Prayer office or close with appropriate words or ceremony. It may be appropriate to use a collect prayer and to say the words of the grace or to use endings from other prayer books.

Saturdays & Kingdom

O God, you are my God, earnestly I seek you;
my soul thirsts for you, my body longs for you, in a dry land where
there is no water.
Who is it that we seek?
We seek God: Who was & is & is to come.
Let's seek God with all our heart?
Amen. God be our centre.
Let's seek God with all our soul?
Amen. God be our vision.
Let's seek God with all our strength?
Amen. God be our wisdom.

Your word O Lord, is a lamp to our feet and a light to our path.
Sustain us according to your promise and we shall live.

The Psalmody

On Saturdays In the Kingdom season.

*Week 1 & Sunday: 33, 117 Week 2 & Monday: 139, 150. Week 3 & Tuesday: 116,
146. Week 4 & Wednesday: 65, 147. 13-end . Week 5 & Thursday: 145, 148. Week 6
& Friday: 23, 125, 147. 1-12 Week 7 & Saturday: 92, 97, 149*

My soul faints with longing for your salvation,
and in your word have I put my hope.

Reading[s]

The word be that goes out from God's mouth shall not return empty,
it shall accomplish God's purpose,
and succeed in what it is sent to do.

Reflection individually or together.

Canticle of the day may be used or a hymn.

Great and Wonderful
Great and wonderful are your deeds, Lord God the Almighty.
Just and true are your ways, O ruler of the nations.
Who shall not revere and praise your name, O Lord? for you alone are
holy.

All nations shall come and worship in your presence: for your just dealings have been revealed.
To the One who sits on the throne and to the Lamb be blessing and honour and glory and might, for ever and ever. Amen.

[Revelation 15.3,4]

After the canticle either continue with a Lord's Prayer office or close with appropriate words or ceremony. It may be appropriate to use a collect prayer and to say the words of the grace or to use endings from other prayer books.

Matters for Further Development.

I am aware as I draw to the close of writing and editing, that there are various things that either couldn't be dealt with in time or which simply deserve to be looked at at a future date. There are some things which it would be nice to do more about. Since this is a book linked to the hope of further discussion on the web, I suspect to mention some of the things I am thinking further about might serve to open up discussion and sharing on the growing edge of reflection.

The offices of prayer could do with further ideas both for the content of what is already in the book and for new offices. It might be good to have forms for midday prayer and for a 'nightcap' office in the style of compline or night prayer. I would like also to be able to have some more seasonal offices such as midsummer, harvest and so on.

I have increasingly come to feel that the metaphor for God implicit in the body prayer in this book could do with supplementing. It tends to 'place' God above us and so perpetuates, for some people unhelpfully, a kind of sky-god transcendent idea of God. If we could find other gestural and positional metaphors which don't metaphorically position God 'above' us it would be a very positive development.

In a more theological mode, I am aware of not having really thought through the relationship of Trinitarian prayer to the Lord's prayer especially in terms of addressing God. This is not to say that the Lord's Prayer is not Trinitarian nor the preceding offices. The address to the Father implies 'in the Son, by the Spirit'. However, it would be good to think further about prayers addressing Christ and the Holy Spirit and how we think and use those -if at all- in a Lord's Prayer approach to prayer. And if we do not use them, how we see the enterprise of praying the Lord's Prayer in relation to them and the traditions they represent.. I am aware of the possibility that one reason for the comparative neglect in devotional and liturgical history of the Lord's Prayer pattern, may be linked to the unfolding of Trinitarian thinking and associated prayer forms.

I have felt too that the work on prayer groups using the Lord's prayer is thin. I have not been in many groups where we have tried to use the pattern aside from set-prayer liturgical settings. I would be glad to hear of experiences of trying to use the Lord's Prayer to structure prayer meetings and similar assemblies. For many groups one of the big challenges of trying to do this is self-discipline in the face of so much practice and experience of praying together informally without that kind of structure.

To be sure, there are structures which normally organise such meetings, but they are different and usually unacknowledged, being assumed to be spontaneous. So it is also important that we make explicit the hidden assumptions of group prayer so that we can keep them or change them according to the needs and aims of the group. I am currently working on some writing that relates to this somewhat. Perhaps that will help.

Thanks, respect and kudos due

This book has been in the process of writing for a long time. It is not trivial to say that in one respect it has been a lifetime in the making. I was taught to pray the Lord's prayer at home and in school and later in Churches and Christian Unions and other Christian societies. So respect is given to my mother, my teachers and the innumerable people who have prayed with me and for me.

Terry Virgo speaking on his book Praying the Lord's Prayer at St.Thomas Crookes in Sheffield in the mid 1980's was a huge influence and thanks are due to him and to Robert Warren, then vicar of St.Thomas's for encouraging me in company with thousands to look at the 'Our Father' as a pattern prayer.

A special thanks also to Sue Wallace of the Visions community in York who included the body prayer in her book on creative prayer and set me to realising that perhaps some of these ideas and perspectives should be published so that they would be available to a wider audience.

More personally I thank my family for putting up with my absence as I wrote these pages and especially to my wife, Tracy Reynolds for reading the nearly-finished result and making helpful comments. I also remain grateful to Liz Hoare for her encouragement and to the Grove Books Spirituality Series editorial group for encouraging me to write even though in the end what I wrote turned out to be something they couldn't use.

I would also like to thank Arun Arora, Judy Drummond, Matthew Knox, Matthew Watts, and Justine Woolley for their help on the pictorial aspects of this book.

Further Reading.

In this section I have tried to collect together details of books articles and websites that have been influential in the writing of this book or that I think will be helpful in following up some of the ideas or themes.

Books on prayer

Bradshaw, Paul. Two Ways of Praying, Introducing Liturgical Spirituality. SPCK, London, 1995. 0281047995

Guiver, George. Company of Voices: Daily Prayer and the People of God. Canterbury Press. 2001. 1853113948

Heppenstall-West, Annie. Reclaiming the Sealskin. Meditations in the Celtic Spirit. Wild Goose Publications, Glasgow. 2002. 1901557669

Jeremias, Joachim , & Bowden J (Translator). Prayers of Jesus. .SCM Press. 1967.

Warren, Robert. An Affair of the Heart, How to Pray More Effectively. Highland Books. Guildford 1994. 1 897913 09 5

Wallace, Sue. Multi-sensory Prayer: Over 60 Innovative Ready-to-use Ideas. Scripture Union Publishing. 2000. 1859994652.

This book includes a version of the body prayer based on the Lord's Prayer pattern which is (correctly) attributed to me.

Books on the Lord's Prayer.

Jeremias, Joachim. The Lord's Prayer. Fortress Press 1964.

Migliore, Daniel L (ed). The Lord's Prayer, Persepctives for reclaiming Christian Prayer. Eerdmans, Grand Rapids MI.1993.

Slack, Kenneth. Praying the Lord's Prayer Today. SCM Press, London. 1973. 334 01289 9

Stevenson, Kenneth. Abba Father. Understanding and Using the Lord's Prayer. Canterbury Press, Norwich 2000. 1 85311 382 4

Virgo, Terry. Praying the Lord's Prayer. Word Publishing. 1987.

Books on spiritual direction, spiritual-life coaching and soul friendship

Hart, Thomas N,. The Art of Christian Listening. Mahwah, NJ, Paulist Press. 1980. 0-8091-2345-2

Jeff, Gordon,. Spiritual Direction for Every Christian. London, SPCK. 1987. 0-281-04318-3

Long, Anne. Approaches to Spiritual Direction. Grove Books, Cambridge, 2005 [4th ed]. ISBN: 1 85174 072 4

Millar, Harold. Finding a Personal Rule of Life. Grove Books, Cambridge. 1987, 2003. ISBN: 1 85174 053 8

Simpson, Ray. Soul Friendship, Celtic Insights into Spiritual Mentoring. London, Hodder & Stoughton.1999. 0-340-73548-1

Prayer Books

A New Zealand Prayer Book: He Karakia Mihinare O Aotearoa ISBN: 006060199X

David Stancliffe and Brother Tristram SSF (editors). Celebrating Common Prayer. Continuum International Publishing Group. Mowbray. 1992

Northumbria Community. Celtic Daily Prayer from the Northumbria Community. ISBN 0551032669

The United Reformed Church of Great Britain. Worship: from the United Reformed Church. The United Reformed Church, London, 2003. 0853462194

Some web links

http://www.embody.co.uk/labyrinth/online.html -an online labyrinth

http://www.aidan.org.uk/ is the site for guidelines on a 'way' of life.

http://www.christian-ecology.org.uk -helpful on environmental issues.

http://www.lifestyle-movement.org.uk/ -lots of lifestyle ideas.

http://www.globalissues.org/ -food for thought about the big picture.

http://www.wearewhatwedo.org/ -ideas for more just and generous living

http://sdiworld.org/index.pl/what_is_spiritual_direction2.html A way in to thinking about spiritual direction etc.

http://www.theforgivenessproject.com/ -site with stories of forgiveness.

http://mb-soft.com/believe/txs/prayer.htm -prayer in general

http://www.cofe.anglican.org/worship/ Resources for liturgy from the Church of England.

http://abbeynous.schtuff.com/ -the site that goes with this book.

Index